by Eric Greinke

Poetry
Sand & Other Poems
Caged Angels
The Last Ballet
Iron Rose
The Broken Lock - Selected Poems 1960-1975
Selected Poems 1972-2005
Wild Strawberries
Traveling Music
For The Living Dead - New & Selected Poems

Translation
The Drunken Boat & Other Poems From The French Of
        Arthur Rimbaud

Collaborations
Great Smoky Mountains (with Ronnie Lane)
Masterpiece Theater (with Brian Adam)
Up North (with Harry Smith)
Get It (with Mark Sonnenfeld)
Catching The Light - 12 Haiku Sequences (with John Elsberg)
Beyond Our Control - Two Collaborative Poems (with Hugh Fox)
All This Dark - 24 Tanka Sequences (with John Elsberg)

Essays & Interviews
The Potential Of Poetry
Conversation Pieces

Creative Non-fiction
The Art Of Natural Fishing

Fiction
Sea Dog - A Coast Guard Memoir

Social Commentary
Whole Self / Whole World - Quality Of Life In The 21st Century

Poets In Review

Eric Greinke

PRESA PRESS
Rockford, MI

Cover montage (*left to right*): *bottom row:* Ed Ochester, Lyn Lifshin, Donald Hall; *2nd row:* Charles Bukowski, Hélène Sanguinetti; Robert Creeley; *3rd row:* Lynne Savitt, Gerald Locklin, Nikki Giovanni; *top row:* Robert Bly, Jerome Rothenberg, Diane Wakoski.

First Edition

Printed in the United States of America

ISBN: 978-0-9965026-0-3

Library of Congress Control Number: 2015943748

PRESA PRESS
PO Box 792   Rockford MI 49341
presapress@aol.com   www.presapress.com

Contents

Introduction

I wrote my first review of a poetry book in 1972, at the age of twenty-four. I was invited to write reviews for *The Grand Rapids Sunday Press* by their Book Editor Wes Wietsma, based on my literary activism in the Western Michigan area. This was a period in which I'd begun to publish poetry in national literary magazines and organize many local poetry readings. I was the founder and editor of *Amaranthus*, the first university-sponsored literary magazine of Grand Valley State University. I participated in the Michigan Artists in the Schools program, introducing students from elementary to high school age to contemporary poetry and using the writing exercises developed by poet Kenneth Koch in his ground-breaking book *Wishes, Lies And Dreams: Teaching Children to Write Poetry* (1970). I had also published three small chapbooks and two full-length poetry collections (*Sand & Other Poems*, 1971, and *Caged Angels*, 1972) at that point.

Another qualification for becoming a reviewer was that I had participated the previous year in week-long poetry workshops with two of the leading avant-garde poets of that time, namely Robert Bly and Ted Berrigan. I had attended readings by a large number of the most important poets of the generation previous to my own, including Beat poets Allen Ginsberg, Gregory Corso, Diane di Prima and Lawrence Ferlinghetti; Black Mountain poets Robert Creeley, Joel Oppenheimer and Paul Blackburn; Black poets Sonia Sanchez, Nikki Giovanni, Etheridge Knight, Dudley Randall, Al Young and Herbert Woodward Martin; experimental poets Armand Schwerner, Anselm Hollo and Jackson MacLow; deep imagists James Wright and Robert Kelly; confessional poets Diane Wakoski and John Logan, and others. Although writing book reviews wasn't my own idea, I wrote over a hundred of them over two ten-year periods separated by thirty-two years, represented by sections one and two of this selection.

That *The Grand Rapids Press*, a general-interest

newspaper of Michigan's second largest city, should run a series of reviews of poetry books, many of which were published by small, non-commercial literary presses, is significant. The early seventies was a time when poetry actually appealed to a wider audience. There was even a popular song, *Poetry Man*, recorded by singer Phoebe Snow. The mimeo revolution that began in the mid and late sixties had been one of the major factors that influenced the public. College poetry readings were frequent and well-attended. Today, nostalgic Boom Generation poets refer to that period as a 'golden age.'

We face a much different situation today. While the gross number of poetry readers has increased by quite a bit, the ironic fact is that the percentage of the population that reads poetry has actually decreased significantly. Presumably, this effect is due to the population explosion of the past forty years.

The Grand Rapids Sunday Press had a wide circulation. I used to get it on newsstands when I lived way up north on the Keweenaw Peninsula, near the Canadian border. A half-million copies of my reviews were printed when they were in *The Grand Rapids Press*. These were generally five hundred word pieces. (I received $50.00 each for them.) Section One of this book contains twenty pieces from the first decade.

Section Two contains twenty-six reviews from the second decade, which commenced in 2005. These are generally lengthier than the newspaper reviews. *The Pedestal Magazine* was the publisher of several of these second decade pieces. *The Pedestal* reviews run to one thousand words each. *The Pedestal Magazine* is an eclectic, online literary journal. It gets twenty-eight thousand 'qualified' readers per issue. Sometimes my reviews have been reprinted in subsequent issues, which of course doubled their worldwide circulation.

Three of the reviews (Linda Lerner, Lyn Lifshin and Gloria Mindock) were written for the *Home Planet News*, a literary tabloid out of New York. A thousand copies are distributed free through NYC bookstores. These reviews are a hybrid of the newspaper and literary magazine styles, since

HPN is really both.

A number of reviews were also written for *Presa* magazine, an eclectic literary magazine edited by Roseanne Ritzema, Hugh Fox, Harry Smith and myself. Its circulation was five hundred copies, typical for an independent literary magazine. I note that my reviews which were written for small-circulation literary magazines (i.e. reviews of Donald Hall, Robert Bly, and David Chorlton) tended toward greater exuberance and less self-discipline. Obviously, professional standards are different for a literary audience as opposed to a general one.

I also reviewed several short chapbook collections in *Presa*. These reviews ranged in length from one hundred-fifty to three hundred words. The short form review is particularly well-suited to chapbooks, because they are more compressed and precise than longer reviews. Sometimes, as in the cases of Gerald Locklin, Mark Sonnenfeld and Guy Beining, I reviewed two of the poet's chapbooks together, to provide a 'mini-overview.'

Most of the books I reviewed were assigned to me by an editor, though a few were generated by me from books that small publishers sent me. This was the case, for example, with Charles Bukowski's second poetry collection *Mocking-Bird Wish Me Luck*. I had a correspondence with the publisher, John Martin, of the Black Sparrow Press in Los Angeles, California. The resulting review was the first big newspaper review Bukowski received. I reviewed a number of Black Sparrow and other small press books during that first decade.

When I read what I wrote in my twenties, I see that from the very beginning, I chose to identify both strengths and weaknesses in the books I reviewed. I wanted the reviews to be realistic and balanced. Sometimes this approach resulted in less-than-favorable reviews, such as the reviews of Richmond Lattimore and Robert Creeley. Though I had an acquaintance with Creeley and liked his earlier work, I felt obligated to provide an honest response to his book *A Day Book*, which I thought was *too* interiorized, even for him. Creeley was a master who had taken a direction that made his already obscure work even more so.

Despite the thirty-two year time gap between my two periods of reviewing poetry books, I continued to take a balanced approach, identifying what I thought were both strengths and weaknesses of each collection. Even so, the majority of the reviews are positive. A review of any poetry book promotes poetry itself. I've tried to identify those poets who have achieved a certain level of awareness as masters of their craft. I think it's a reviewer's job to give honest feedback. From the beginning, I have also included whole sample poems from the books under review, on the premise that there is no substitute for letting poems speak for themselves.

In my second decade of reviewing, from my late fifties to my present age of sixty-seven, the knowledge gap was greatly reduced. Those reviews are marked by a more accepting attitude toward different poetic approaches. I had become an eclectic reader in the intervening years. As such, my reviews sought to discover the premise of each poet's approach rather than judge it from a set of external standards. When evaluating a book, I studied it with several readings and asked myself if the poet was successful in fulfilling his/her goals. Having received over one hundred reviews of my own books, from all over the world, I have learned how it feels to be understood and have wished to return the favor. If there is something that needs negative criticism in one of my own poetry collections, I sincerely want to know. Out of respect, I have assumed that my fellow poets feel the same way.

Finally, the reviews I've selected for inclusion in this book continue to represent my sincere thoughts. In the mutual interest of both the reader and myself, I have left out the reviews that no longer represent my opinion, or are too over-the-top to be considered balanced criticism. My opinions have not always reflected the prevailing ones, but at least they contained honest reactions by whoever I was at the time of their composition. Our ultimate loyalty should be to poetry itself, which can only benefit from an honest examination of its issues.

Eric Greinke

ONE

Speech Acts & Happenings
by Robert Vas Dias
(Bobbs-Merrill Press, Indianapolis, IN)

This is an important volume of poetry. Longer than the average poetry collection (106 pages), Robert Vas Dias' new book covers a wide spectrum of modern experience. The poems range from short, restricted Korean sijo to longer and freer forms.

Flexibility is the most impressive aspect of the collection, although generally the poet handles longer poems with more ease, seeming to find his voice more readily when he is not being held in by the restrictions of shorter forms.

Vas Dias is poet-in-residence at Grand Valley State College.

The book is arranged in the manner of the best poetry collections — that is, rather than being just a hodge-podge of unrelated poems, it is programmed into smaller books within the larger. Taken together, these sections give the collection an integrity that a less organized book might lack.

The first section is entitled "Speech Acts." The high points of the section are "Sailing Twenty Years After," a poem to the poet's father on his deathbed, and "On Cutting Open a Friend's Book," dedicated to poet Toby Olson. The weak point here is "Returned Marine." The problem is that the poem is too obvious, displaying the rather time-worn tendency of "social protest" poetry to object to regimentation.

The second section is called "Urban Crisis." The first poem, of the same name, is a very strong work and the longest in the book. Its design and rhythm is similar to Allen Plantz's excellent "A Night for Rioting." This section is strong, with much of the strength provided by such poems as "Urban Metaphor," "My Fight Against Crime," and "What Happened."

The third and middle section is the weakest, although it does have its highlights. Its title is "Some Space Poems." In his concern over tautness and workability, Vas Dias sometimes makes the poem too obvious, giving the reader something he likely would rather gain on his own. This problem exists mostly in the shorter works, though some of the longer ones, most notably "July 21, 1969," are handled very well.

In the fourth section, "15 Sijo of Situation," Vas Dias overcomes his earlier problem with shorter forms. There is none of the obvious in these subtle and gentle little poems. The sijo is a Korean form that consists of six lines and between 45 and 50 syllables. Vas Dias does not always stick to the syllable restriction, but it is to his credit that he experiments with the ancient form, giving it a fresh twist with such fine works as "Auto Sijo" and "Subway Sijo."

There is a great deal of pleasure to be found in the next section, "Pleasure & the Naming of It." This is another strong section containing what is perhaps the best poem in the book, "The Greenness of the Burma Jade World." If not the best, the poem is certainly the most lyrical, once again showing the poet's flexibility.

In the last section of this multi-colored book, called "Confrontation," many earlier concerns find their answers. Here too one discovers that the cover drawing (beautifully done by artist Bob Hart of Lamont) is related to the poetry, landscapes being a prevalent image in this section.

The book ends with a poem entitled "Revolutionary," and this is a good word to describe the book. It isn't as revolutionary as, say, the new York School of poetry, but that is good – because Vas Dias knows enough to hold on to the good things of the past while at the same time breaking into the future. It's a fine book. I recommend it to anyone who is interested in the new direction of American poetry.

A Caterpillar Anthology - A Selection Of Poetry And Prose From Caterpillar Magazine
edited by Clayton Eshleman
(Doubleday-Anchor Press, New York, NY)

If you are interested in comparatively recent developments in contemporary poetry, this anthology is for you. The book is some 500 pages of works selected from the first 12 issues of the now-defunct "Caterpillar," one of this nation's most ambitious and valuable literary periodicals. (I hesitate to call it a "magazine" because it was more like a continuing anthology such as Michigan's own "Sumac.")

Although there is a predominance of the "Black Mountain School" of poets (projective-verse) represented, there is a wide variety of poets including Dianne Wakoski, Jackson MacLow, Paul Blackburn, Jerome Rothenberg, David Antlin, Robert Kelly, Robin Blaser and Charles Olson. In this sense, it justifies its title of "anthology."

Most of the book is poetry, but it also contains some fiction and criticism including one of the best extended film reviews I've ever read – Richard Grossinger's review of "The Graduate." Grossinger's historic perspective is very revealing. Even though he finds the movie to be impossibly trite, he sees the two main characters emerging victoriously in the end, with the film behind them as a sort of picture of "how it is" most of the time. Benjamin's use of the steel cross to bar the church door, for example, is seen by Grossinger not as a symbol of anything, but simply the use of the handiest object available.

Most of the poetry is solid and distributed at the level of "above average." A number of the poems are distinctly superior.

"Night Walk" by Jackson MacLow is a major work in which he succeeds in reducing the language to its most elemental and powerful form. Other notable poems include Diane Wakoski's "I Have Had to Learn to Live With My Face," Robert Duncan's "Rites of Participation" and Armand Schwerner's "Tablet VIII."

Schwerner's work especially has great satiric and comic value. His self-parody is at a high level, and his "translator's notes" make you wonder how you could ever have taken Eliot's notes to "The Wasteland" seriously. The book also includes other, more serious, poems by Schwerner, and his contributions alone make the anthology worth buying.

There are weak places, as might be expected of such a large volume, yet in general this is an amazingly fine look at what went on in the not-too-deep underground two years back. It would be difficult for a book of this kind to have as its origin the deep underground, since widespread publications such as this tend to force the truly avant-garde further away.

Publications like "Caterpillar" constitute an "establishment" of their own, and the writers who publish in them are those who will be studied as the "major poets" within the next 10 years.

It's a process that should be speeded up, so that future generations of poets will not have to grow old or die before they are "discovered" by the reading public.

Discover this book. You'll be glad you did.

The Yellow Room - Love Poems
by Donald Hall
(Harper & Row, New York, NY)

Reading Donald Hall's most recent work, *The Yellow Room*, (subtitled *Love Poems*), I am aware that he is now a mature poet who has found his strength with a new voice. There is a calmness in this book that could only be conveyed by a poet with Hall's maturity. His new poems have none of the unnecessary tension-for-its-own-sake with which we have all become so weary. Rather, the tone is conversational:

> You have called me
> a baked potato.
> Very well, then.
> I would like to be eaten
> by someone as pretty
> as a wooden
> propeller, like you   (page 5)

undramatic & personal. In one respect, these poems represent a departure for Hall from his previous control. While his earlier poems displayed a superb craftsmanship & technical orientation, often they lacked the humor, anger & compassion which is now most apparent. The problem was due largely to an over-emphasis on formality & unity. The problem no longer exists. In *The Yellow Room* Hall's wit & sensitivity are allowed, even encouraged, to shine through. There is a casual freedom that never really came through in his earlier work.

The freedom is exhilarating & fresh. The poems give the impression of having been written as they happened, perhaps in a diary. If you read the book from cover to cover, there is a narrative movement that is not unlike the plot line of a novel. You follow the love affair from its beginning in the yellow room to its inevitable ending, with the speaker alone. Much of the tonal color is accomplished through the poet's capable usage of gold & yellow images:

> The grass moves,
> it grows taller, summer lengthens
> gold days.
> (page 3)

> Pale gold of the walls, gold
> of the centers of daisies, yellow roses
> pressing from a clear bowl. All day
> we lay on the bed,
> (from *Gold,* page 14)

& so on. The color follows the lovers through the book, appearing when they are together, being replaced by stones when they separate. After a breakup & makeup:

> Three months.
> So we are lovers again.
> Yet we will do everything again.
> The grass moves,
> it grows taller, summer lengthens
> gold days.
> (page 51 - in full)

Note the restated theme: an almost musical kind of repetition. The image of the stone appears & re-appears too. The stones seem to represent the speaker's solitude & love. They are there when he is alone:

> The lake enormous and calm;
> a stone falls;
> for an hour the surface
> moves, holding to itself the frail
> shudders of its skin. Stones
> on the dark bottom
> make the lake calm,
> the life worth living.   (from *Waters,* page 28)

The symbols all appear & re-appear like the gold. One poem, named *The Recurrent Dream,* is the image of death without love. This theme is restated during the last section of the book. (After the final breakup of the two lovers.)

The image of the stone becomes the central image at the end. The book finishes with a poem called *The Stones* (quoted in full):

Now it is gone, all of it.
No, it is there,
a rock island twelve miles offshore
in the Atlantic. Straight cliffs,
salt grass on top,
rabbits, snipe.

At lowest tide,
a scrap of sand; maybe once a year
the sea is so calm
that an island man breaches his coracle,
wedges the anchor in stone,
and rock-climbs to the top.

He traps small game,
listening to the wind, fearful
of skull island.
Monks in the middle ages
lived in a stone house here
whole lives.
(The Stones, page 74)

It is an excellent & powerful collection: one that is subtle & graceful without lacking power. It is the work of a mature & sensitive man: perhaps Michigan's best older poet. It is a book of love. I recommend it, because that is what we need most.

.

Shaking The Pumpkin - Traditional Poetry Of The Indian North Americas

edited by Jerome Rothenberg

(Doubleday-Anchor Press, New York, NY)

This large and significant volume, subtitled "Traditional Poetry Of The Indian North Americas," has been awaited with eager anticipation by poets the world over ever since Jerome Rothenberg announced that he would be doing a companion book to his highly acclaimed effort of 1968 entitled "Technicians Of The Sacred."

"Technicians" was a similarly large volume that dealt with tribal poetries on a more general and worldwide plane, being subtitled "A Range Of Poetries From Africa, America, Asia And Oceania."

It established Rothenberg as the foremost American poet working with so-called "primitive" and magical traditions.

The fact that the true role of the poet is that of "shaman" or prophet is nowhere more apparent than in "Shaking The Pumpkin."

These translations of Indian poems and ritualistic songs often are incantory or mystical in nature, giving them at the same time a simplicity and a power that is unmatched by most of the weak and highly controlled poetry of today (especially that being written in the universities).

In a "post-face" at the back of the book, Rothenberg makes the following statement:

"I am not doing this for the sake of curiosity, but have smoked a pipe to the powers from whom these songs came, and I ask them not to be offended with me for singing these songs which belong to them."

The strongest section in the book is that titled "A

Book of Extensions (1)."

This section departs from the verbal – including conceptional, pictorial and graphic mediums. It is stronger than the rest of the book because it seems to communicate more directly the essence of the poetic experience. The Indian poetry is perhaps more purely translated through non-verbal means, it being essentially an oral tradition.

My only criticism of the book is that the individual translators do not shed their individual styles, as I believe they should have in order for the translations to be more pure. I was able, after reading only the first hundred pages or so, to identify each translator from a reading of the poems or songs. Although this may be (is) a good trait in the writing of original poetry, I find it irritating when reading what is supposed to be a true representation of the poetry of another race of people.

Too often the workings are essentially laden down with contemporary structures and forms which I simply can't believe the Indians would have used. This criticism is tempered somewhat, however, by the fact that the translations still are "good" poems. It's just that I'm not always sure just who the real author of the work is, the translator or the original poet.

But the book is truly remarkable, and well worth the difficulty encountered in reading it.

Rothenberg has succeeded admirably in "setting poetry back" to where it should have stayed in the first place: the poet as priest and the poem as a window into worlds that are beyond any "civilized" logic or morality.

Smudging
by Diane Wakoski
(Black Sparrow Press, Los Angeles, CA)

At first glance, this new collection of poems by Diane Wakoski brings to mind the line every reviewer seems to repeat regarding her work: "Wakoski is a poet of the 'confessional mode': that group of American poets who have followed in the footsteps of men such as Robert Lowell" ...etc..etc. A closer look reveals that there is much more to her work than meets the eye – perhaps even something new and avant-garde.

The best of Diane Wakoski's poems are successful combinations of two of the more or less "classical" forms: the lyric and the dramatic. It is this marriage of methodology and form that makes her avant-garde.

Her poems begin with the traditional lyric point of view: the first person persona. And indeed, there is no denying that many of the works are nothing more than better-than-average lyric poems, written, indeed, from the "confessional" stance that is so popular today particularly among female writers. But on occasion she stretches the persona of the poem until it detaches itself, and creates something altogether different – and very good, too. When this happens, the personae become dramatic characters. As often as not, this too rises to a yet higher realm of thought: symbolism.

One of the best examples to be found of her use of symbolism is the fine poem entitled "Children Visit the Island." The poem is projected through dramatic setting and through dialogue. The first stanza gives the setting:

"When the children had ferried across the river, they climbed out of the boat, wild plums grew on the trees and blackberry vines covered the island, twisting around everything. Parrots said to the children, 'We have seen your bones bleaching on the sand.' The children said, 'Yes, we have felt the sun.'"

In the best of Wakoski's poems, the images themselves take on dramatic roles. Rocks, fire, the sun and the moon – these interact in a way that is magical to behold.

By stressing the symbolism I do not wish to detract from the poems that are lyrical or personal in their range. For example, the reader who has tried in vain to see all of Diane's "Greed" poem will be happy to note that "Smudging" contains parts 3 and 4. If this "confessional mode" was all she wrote, Diane Wakoski would still be one of the best.

"Greed" is both psychologically deep and revealing, perhaps more of the reader than the poet. Indeed, there is not an unsuccessful poem in the book.

"Smudging" is a big book of poetry. For the price of the book you get more than just another beautifully-designed Black Sparrow edition (although you certainly do get that): you get an engaging mind.

Logan Stone
by D. M. Thomas
(Cape Golliard-Grossman Press, London, UK/New York, NY)

A logan stone is a Cornish-granite rock formation whose name is derived from the fact that it actually is two rocks, with one balanced on the other so delicately that it can be "logged" – or caused to move back and forth – often with the slightest touch of the hand.

The title of this second collection of poems by English poet D. M. Thomas reflects the central theme of the book: rootlessness and isolation.

The title poem reveals in microcosm the essential message of Thomas' poetry: "....neither one nor two doomed and unshakable on its point of infinity that is the miracle to be so weak a finger logs it what constant strength what force it takes to be a loganstone you and I what cold applied granite-fire logging on weakness no storm can move us."

The theme is expanded with poems that involve inter-personal and sexual relationships mixed with social events. Thomas insists that private emotions cannot be distinct from public emotions, making his point early in the book in a sequence called "Computer 70: Dreams and Lovepoems."

This is a distinctly avant-garde sequence, the dream poems being fantasies while the love poems are sexual or personal ones. The poems are arranged to contrast with each other and also to work together toward a common goal.

The arrangement is quite successful, although I cannot say that this type of juxtaposition is unique. Certain American poets have worked for years on "Contrapuntal Poetry," the most notable being Herbert Woodward Martin, the black poet who spent a few years in Grand Rapids as Aquinas College's poet-in-residence.

A further look into the book reveals poems that are ...well, perfect.

These tend to overshadow the beginning sequence. They often are poems that blend religious and sexual symbols together in a way that is nothing short of dazzling. This is especially true of what seems the best poem in the book, entitled "Apocrypha."

Thomas has a control of lyricism and emotion that reminds me of the best work of John Logan. He often includes such normally avoided techniques as end-rhyme and syllabic-structure in his poems, as Logan has done.

I wish to make a point here regarding the book's design. It detracts from the poetry. Surely it would not be asking too much for the publishers to include page numbers and a table of contents? Such a fine poet deserves better treatment. Also, the book contains three photographs, two of which are totally unrelated to the poetry.

Hopefully the publishers' mistakes will not keep readers away from a fine book. Thomas is the best contemporary English poet I've yet read. He doesn't seem content to copy the Americans, as so many other English poets are doing today. His poetry is better than good. It is excellent, and most intriguing.

The Whispering Wind - Poetry By Young American Indians
edited by Terry Allen
(Doubleday-Anchor Press, New York, NY)

Subtitled "Poetry By Young American Indians," this anthology was collected from works written by a group of budding young Indian poets at the Institute of American Indian Arts.

For the most part, the poetry is rather similar to that which is written by most students – rhetorical, awkward and unsophisticated. There are, however, a few young poets of great potential and ability represented in the book.

Liz Schappy has a very well-written work entitled "The Indian Market" in which she proves herself to be a poet of some talent. She has a breathless line that is really quite a fine piece of writing in this poem: "Quick! Look about! No one is near. That tree, that leafy branch, it blackens my hair, makes it grow. That other tree, with red buds hanging, we will drink it for our sweating bodies."

Another young poet I find most appealing is Ted Palmanteer. He is one to watch in the future. Surprisingly enough, his poems do not deal with the same topics most of the others seem to be hung up on. His poetry stands on its own, with the fact that he happens to be an Indian mere frosting on the cake.

I like his "Hit!," and also these lines from "Spring Dew": "I must spring into space. Bleep, bleep at the moon; Spend my springtime drive against eternity then die complete."

Donna Whitewing scores heavily with her poem: "A Vegetable, I Will Not Be." Her work includes a sense of humor – a quality often lacking in young poets.

Others I found enjoyable and rewarding were

Agnes T. Pratt, Gray Cohoe and Ronald Rogers, whose work is the most impressive in the book.

Rogers has a very fine poem entitled "Taking Off" that reminds me of Al Lee. His work is also the most contemporary in the book, which tends to make me think that he has been writing poetry longer than the others.

In general, the book is worthwhile if slightly uneven. It's hard for an anthology that is made up of student works to be of consistent quality, and I think the Institute of American Indian Arts should be commended for producing so many good writers.

If these young poets will continue to work and grow into their creative talents, American literature will certainly benefit from it.

Mocking-Bird Wish Me Luck
by Charles Bukowski
(Black Sparrow Press, Los Angeles, CA)

Charles Bukowski is in the forefront of the underground movement in American poetry. This thick volume of verse, beautifully designed for Black Sparrow Press by Barbara Martin, will give you some idea of why he is so popular.

The poetry is easy-going and generally strong. Bukowski has no use for any of the traditional techniques of poetry. These are replaced with his own speech-like rhythms and tones. The only traditional thing about Bukowski's work is his over-emphasis on himself as a symbol of the times - a preoccupation he shares with a great many of his contemporaries.

Indeed, his poetry is at its best when the poet's ego is somewhere in the background. Poems such as "The Mockingbird" and "Rain" are Bukowski at his finest. Others of the poems, although they may not be failures, can be a bit irritating because the poet tries to force his opinions on the reader.

Some of the poems suffer from too much rhetorical advice. Bukowski proclaims himself the great master all too often, as in poems "The White Poets" and "The Black Poets."

But, egocentrism is what makes him vital and interesting, and indeed he is interesting, and vital, too. At his best he is a clever and stimulating poet; at his worst, he is exactly what most of his readers want him to be: the stereotyped underground poet, such as they might wish themselves to be.

This fact is undoubtedly the key to his success. His is the kind of poetry that thrives best in the underground. No one who has been on the scene for very long can deny that too much underground publishing is done more for egocentric reasons than literary ones. And thus we have a book to consider that is uneven and varied in literary quality.

But, it's a good book, worth reading if only for its best part, which is the section entitled II. "spider on the wall: why do you take so long?" Editing seems to be Bukowski's main problem, and if he would separate his personal poems from his public ones, I think he would have something there.

Poems From Three Decades
by Richmond Lattimore
(Scribner Publishing, New York, NY)

A new package has been sent down from Olympia in the form of this monstrous volume (274 pages) of academic verses by Richmond Lattimore. Lattimore wrote poetry in a consistent manner for 30 years, never changing his style, never giving up iambic pentameter and end-rhyme – never, in short, achieving anything above or below mediocrity. Careful editing would have reduced the size of this book by 80 per cent.

With a volume of this nature, where the poetry is reactionary and rigid, it is hard, indeed often impossible, to get to the content of the poems. Their hearts have been removed, for the most part, by the razor-edge of what is called "craftsmanship" or maybe "technical control." The true value of any poem is that part of it that the poet never intended, or meant to put in. Sadly, with the kind of poetry written by Lattimore and his colleagues, the value of the unintended has been "polished" out.

This is a book that is characteristic of those put out by academic poets. It is filled with the dull, pretentious, self-conscious postures they all are so famous for: literary allusions, poems written after other poems or after paintings or sculptures, poems alluding to the Greeks, "experiments" in rhyme, etc.

The result is a poetry that is hard to read, unenjoyable, dull, and even sometimes downright offensive.

The essential criticism I have to offer is this: turning the pages of this book, one sees no growth or development. The poems at the end are pretty much the same as those at the beginning.

Moving
by Tom Raworth
(Cape Golliard-Grossman Press, London, UK/New York, NY)

This collection of poems by Tom Raworth proceeds with humorous intent and circular direction. Raworth is a British poet who has forsaken the tradition that usually goes with that title to adopt the ideals of the late "New York School." He has made the spiritual crossing completely and honestly.

His book has the "New York School" look with a cover and book design by Joe Brainard, who is one of that group's best and most energetic painters. The poems adopt the look as well with the poet appearing quite calm and comfortable with his scattered composition by field (a technique the New Yorkers picked up from their close allies, the "Projective Verse" people: Creeley, Olsen, Duncan and the Black Mountain gang.)

The poems are very serious, although they may at first appear trivial. Raworth is attempting to make myths out of everyday objects and occurrences. By doing so, he is successful in getting to the roots of things which would perhaps be ignored by most people (poets included) as they speed through their lives.

Sometimes he expresses his inability to name his feelings by creating a vacuum in the poems. One poem, entitled "8:06 p.m., June 10th, 1970" has the following complete text: "poem." Although that may seem insane or worthless at first glance, it is actually an attempt to ask an important question: What exactly belongs in a poem, and what actual meaning is there in the naming of things?

Most of the poems in the book are fuller, more eloquent expressions than that rather extreme example. He succeeds in most cases in putting wonder and excitement into his poems, and that is a very fine thing.

This book is worthwhile reading for those who are

interested in words for their own sake – and in silence. You get a sensation as the book progresses of writing it yourself, working with the poet to create one long poem from all the little things you had forgotten about. Coming full circle, you see that his poems are so meaningless that they are filled with implied meaning.

The Blue Cat
by F. D. Reeve
(Farrar, Straus & Giroux, New York, NY)

F. D. Reeve's second collection of poetry is a complex and sometimes uneven book. His style ranges from heavily-structured Frostian verse to loosely-knit poetry in the American idiom. He is more successful with the latter. His long-lined poems tend to be weighted with extraneous verbiage, whereas shorter lines give him the light look that goes well with his humor and his deft imagery.

I would guess (and hope) that the sections are arranged chronologically, since the first section is markedly inferior to the last two. Most of the early poems are conventional, mainstream things. Notable exceptions are "The Rewinding," "Love Affairs" and "Guernica." The best poems in this section are those that are built entirely from images with no obvious metaphors.

The volume's middle section is a single poem entitled "The Anthill," and the book is worth getting for this poem alone. It is a truly masterful work that deals on a superficial level with the life and death of Henry David Thoreau and on a symbolic level with the birth and death of individualism and mysticism in America. The whole gang is present: Emerson, Margaret Fuller, John Brown and Herman Melville. The poem is an evocation of the spirit of Thoreau and of the free-thinking and often Quixotic transcendentalists. It also has a strong political level. A great poem, really.

The last section is called "The Blue Cat," and these are mostly whimsical pieces as seen through the eyes of the mysterious and jaded Blue Cat (the poet, perhaps). The poems are strong and humorous. An earlier religious theme is picked up in these poems, and handled beautifully.

The best poem in this section is the last one, entitled "Communicating with the Beyond." Here the tone is mixed: slightly surreal images such as "Green peppers hang from the purple trees," and strong, elegiac lines such as "I have been in Hell, have seen the black fruit on the black trees" are juxtaposed to create a moving work of art.

For a second book of poetry, I'd say this was pretty good. The poet is sure of himself, and that always helps. The Thoreau poem is perfect, and the worst thing that can be said regarding the worst poems is that they are mediocre.

I suspect that Reeve could overcome any problems he has and make his poetry as consistently good as his fiction, if he would. I for one hope he does as a sense of humor is a rarity among poets.

The Providings
by Carl Thayler
The Revenant
by Dan Gerber
Xeme
by Rebecca Newth
Accidental Center
by Michael Heller
Midwatch
by Keith Wilson
(Sumac Press, Fremont, MI)

The Sumac Press, of Fremont, has published such an excellent group of poetry books in recent months that rather than review only one or two of these, I have decided to review in brief five of what I consider to be the best ones.

"*The Providings,*" by Carl Thayler, covers nine years of his poetry. As can be expected, this makes his book uneven and varied.

Thayler's poetry is relaxing. He speaks in a nice, easy manner that draws you in to hear what he has to say. I liked "The Goodrich Poem," a longer work, best. His poetry is best when the casualness is gently controlled. Any uneven quality in his book is due to a failure to rewrite one last time before publication. Even so, the book is very friendly and very pleasant reading.

"*The Revenant,*" by Sumac editor Dan Gerber, is perhaps the best book on their list. Gerber is an imagist, and I appreciate his keen sense of place, things and events.

The last poem in the book, "Exposures at f/22," is worth the price of the whole collection. In this poem, Gerber does what he does best: He leaves out all obvious poetic metaphor and simply reports the images. This results in a poem of the highest caliber, one that is clean, simple and powerful.

At first, his work may appear low-keyed and insignificant, but if the reader will give these poems his fullest attention, he will come away satisfied that Gerber has found a way to make the smallest things in life seem important.

Rebecca Newth's first book, "*Xeme*," contains several fine poems, all sustained by her ability to reveal her emotions. If a few of the poems do not succeed, it is due to a tightening up, a fear, perhaps, of revealing too much of herself.

Her work shows great promise, though, especially in poems such as "Taking Away a Field of Strawberries" and "Dorothy."

It says something about the seriousness of a press, I think, when they choose to publish as many first books as Sumac has. It is also to their credit that the first books they have done have been such good ones as "*Xeme*."

"*Accidental Center*," by Michael Heller, stands out along with Gerber's book at the top of Sumac's list. Every poem in the book is good. Really good. Heller has much in common with Gerber stylistically. He is not as given to straight images as Gerber is, though. He blends in a more specific personalism than Gerber, the result of which is a more opinionated poetry. But I like it, coming from him.

The poems have a kind of wisdom. The best poem in this book of best poems is "Birds at the Alcazaba." Highly recommended.

"*Midwatch*," by Keith Wilson, is another excellent book. It is supposed to be a collection of single poems but I find it to be one very long poem instead. All the segments work together, like links in a chain, and there are no weak links.

Since I have stood many midwatches (for the uninitiated, it is watch on board ship that lasts from midnight to 4 a.m.) I can identify with Wilson's observations. His style is comfortable and unpretentious. I'd like to say more about this one, but it would involve me in writing a poem just as long as his to go with his, so I won't.

These books and several others published by Sumac Press and by other quality small presses, are vital and valuable. Presses like Sumac publish not for monetary gain, but for love of literature, and as such they deserve our gratitude and support.

A Day Book
by **Robert Creeley**
(Scribner Publishing, New York, NY)

Robert Creeley has the unenviable position in American poetry of being "recognized" as a master in his own lifetime. This is unfortunate for several reasons, not the least of which is the fact that poetry readers and reviewers will be giving Creeley something called "poetic license" with more than the usual restraint and scrutiny. I for one will not.

Creeley gained his early reputation by combining the methods of Charles Olson and his "Composition by Field" with his own subtle feeling for words and images to create a poetry that is much admired and imitated today. His early work often could be identified by its short, spasmodic lines and its novel use of syntactical arrangement. These poems had a primal strength. They were "overpacked" with the poet's own confusions, fears and tension, and they were deserving of their growing audience.

But there seems to be a pattern wherein younger poets of great ability, when recognized too soon, tend to become overconfident and often presumptuous. This is, I greatly fear, the problem with the "new" Robert Creeley.

"*A Day Book*" contains some of the most jumbled, unreadable writing I've been confronted with. Contrary to some critical opinions, his prose has never been particularly readable. He has persisted in a desire to make the writing "unmemorable" with the hope that it will achieve a momentary quality that would change according to the mood of the reader.

The first part of "*A Day Book*" is a section of this kind of ghastly prose titled (surprise!) "A Day Book." This section takes up half the book and is simply (or not so simply) a mental diary of Creeley's days. Although I know he is an interesting man, having spent a week two years ago in his presence, I am bored by this writing.

The rest of the book, titled "In London," is made up of poetry. Although these are definitely more along Creeley's line, they do not, for the most part, succeed as good poems. Occasionally, I come across a line or a poem that reminds me of the old Robert Creeley. He could still do it, if he wanted to. His forte is still the short, concise poem.

But things are too easy for him now. He can get his work published by practically any journal in the world. He is a household word among poets and English teachers, and even among many "nonliterary" readers. He has "made it" but, like Robert Frost and so many others, he has sacrificed his good judgment somewhere along the way. He no longer has to try to get our attention, and thus, loses it.

But he still has mine. I remember the poetry that gave this man his name and his identity, and I will watch his work now and in the future to see if it will return. It hasn't yet, for the most part, in "*A Day Book*," but there are hints, and the big book isn't over yet.

My House
by Nikki Giovanni
(Harper-Perennial, New York, NY)

This is poetry of such magnitude and power that it cannot really be "reviewed," only recommended.

"*My House*," the new collection by beautiful and black Nikki Giovanni, runs the entire possible scale of emotions. She reveals her most personal memories and dreams, next to her political and social convictions, in such an honest and vivid and compelling way that you are drawn in for good. You will never be the same after reading this. It is a revolution of straight talk.

From the foreword by Ida Lewis: "Nikki knows the necessity of remembering, for to remember is to be born again; to forget is to dwell in eternal darkness. She teaches us not only that the people of the past are very much alive, but that we must not judge them from our modern pinnacle of knowledge and awareness. Our ancestors had the attitudes of their time, and Nikki takes them as they were, as they were obliged to be. 'Nobody,' she says,'ever wakes up in the morning and says how can I hurt black people today? Not even white people. People wake up and ask how can I get a little further ahead? We are the only people who will read someone out of the race – the entire nation – because we don't agree with them. That's really crazy when, if we just can assume that others have the integrity we say we possess, we would be that much stronger.' And she vows to go on peering into the shadows of the past. Taking the most anguished of themes and personal experiences, she explores their manifold depths."

And she remembers; and in her remembering she creates an art that is unique and personal and gripping and intelligent.

Other poets could learn a very great deal from her methods. She writes perfectly, using the American language honestly, and building her poems from such sensual images that you relate to her and feel that you know her and love her very deeply.

If you want to know what real poetry is, and if you are never going to read another book of poetry, ever, then this is it. This is the best collection I've read yet.

She is a major poet (and that means human being). And she "...can fly – like a bird in the sky."

John's Heart
by Tom Clark
(Golliard-Grossman Press, London, UK/New York, NY)

The "New York School" strikes again! Yes, "they" are still at it – still insisting that all things are subjects for poetry, and that poems should reflect a moment in time, where the poet constructs a poem in memory of his feelings, and then moves on.

Even though few of the "New York School" live in New York anymore, reviewers like myself still call them that. Even though Frank O'Hara posthumously won the National Book Award for his collected poems two years ago, he is still referred to in a recent review (along with others of his school) as a "clown of the spirit." And, I suspect, what irks the critics and the timid academic poets the most about these people is their persistent infiltration into the consciousness of American poetry.

Tom Clark has been one of the "ring-leaders" of this revolution. Judging from his new book, "*John's Heart*," he will continue in that role. Clark is intensely personal in his approach to cut-up techniques and spatial composition, and his drawings are good, too.

I like these poets because they refuse to stand still, and because their work is so communal, so alive and so totally intelligent. They simply don't care whether or not they are liked, and you have to like them for that.

If I am tending here to discuss the whole school rather than Clark in particular, it is because his book – as with most of their books – is largely a group effort.

These poets often write in collaboration, a technique learned from their painter-friends. Indeed, one of the most charismatic personalities of the school, Ted Berrigan, seem ubiquitous in his influence. "*John's Heart*" is dedicated to Berrigan, and its cover bears a collage-portrait of his distinctive outline.

45

Aside from the drawings and collaborations, "John's Heart" contains several of Clark's new poems. These show him advancing on the foundations of his earlier books, "Stone," "Air," "Smack" and "Green." They focus on single words as concrete images, the result of which is a poem that begins "pony try" and ends "band." This is highly creative work, though some surely will scoff at it.

The influence of Clark's friend Aram Saroyan is apparent, but I think Clark goes beyond Saroyan by attempting more elaborate structures and combinations.

Finally, I think poets like Clark are a good sign of things to come.

"*John's Heart*" is an innovative and important book, and those who come to it with any preconception of what poetry must be will be surprised and unable to cope with it – not because the poetry doesn't work, but because the reader doesn't. This is a book for those seeking welcome relief and many happy returns.

New Work
by Joe Brainard
(Black Sparrow Press, Los Angeles, CA)

This collection of short poems and statements by New York painter and collage-artist Joe Brainard is a refreshing and highly personal book. The author puts himself squarely in the middle of his work, honestly revealing what he is, thinks and does.

The writing is simple and straightforward, without adornment or artifice, and I found myself liking Brainard and his approach a great deal. Reading "*New Work*" is like meeting a new friend.

Brainard has an almost Oriental regard for silence, and appreciation. The shortest poem in this book, entitled "Night," reads 'Day, you have gone / and done it again.'

The scope of this type of writing is somewhat limited, yet is successful, intelligent and entertaining. You do not laugh at Brainard's childlike approach – you laugh in it and with it.

The book reinforces my opinion that the New York poets have accomplished more than any other group during the last decade. For, in one respect, one must look at their work as a reaction to the rigid modes, forms and philosophies of the generation of poets that preceded them, especially the academic poets still in control of college classrooms today.

Brainard has proceeded on the assumption that a poem will only be as interesting as the person who wrote it. Brainard is very interesting.

Last, I would like to note that the book's production and design are exceptional. Black Sparrow is, of course, noted for producing beautiful books, but this time designer Barbara Martin has outdone herself.

TWO

The Winged Energy Of Delight
by Robert Bly
(Harper-Perennial Press, New York, NY)

Robert Bly's massive efforts over the past 50 years to expand American awareness of the international poetry scene is generously sampled in this wonderful anthology & commentary.

I cannot review the individual poets in this space. Suffice it to say that they are poets of world stature: Tomas Tranströmer, Mirabai, Kabir, Antonio Machado, Juan Ramón Jiménez, Francis Ponge, Pablo Neruda, Georg Trakl, Rainer Maria Rilke, Basho, Rolf Jacobsen, Gunnar Ekelöf, Issa, Federico García Lorca, Olav H. Hauge, Harry Martinson, César Vallejo, Miguel Hernandez, Rumi, Horace, Ghalib, & Hafez.

On a personal note, I received Bly's early collection of Kabir, the fifteenth century Indian poet (*The Fish In The Sea Is Not Thirsty*, Lillaberlero Press, 1971.) in 1973, from Bly himself. It is one of my most treasured possessions. That same year, the late Walter Lowenfels introduced me to the work of Nobel laureate Pablo Neruda. In 1981 I got Bly's collection of Rilke (*Selected Poems of Rainer Maria Rilke,* Harper Colophon, 1981.). This book brought Rilke alive for me & I was struck by the lucidity of Bly's running commentary. My copy has become quite worn. I should have gotten the hardcover.

All of Robert Bly's translations were done in a manner analogous to method acting. Bly used "method acting" to *become* Kabir, Rilke & the others. He repeatedly took emotional & conceptual risks, prioritizing the integrity of the imagery, *transmutating* it, rather than producing just another literal translation of the words. He bravely inserted a running commentary, in defiance of literary convention, to *teach* us about the poets & their work, with the deep scholarly integrity that he has become known for.

There is little wonder that Robert Bly is recognized for the depth of his imagery, his subtle tonal control, his profound thoughtfulness & his preternatural ability to explicate universal archetypes & mythological symbols in poetry.

Every poet & poetry reader in America should own every book Robert Bly has written. Short of that, one can meet the minimal requirement by having his selected original poetry & this volume, to "cover" his monumental achievements. A copy of his *Iron John: A Book About Men* (Addison-Wesley, 1990.) is also advisable.

Bly bridges the gap between America & the rest of the world, among other gaps both personal (inter & intra) & universal. American poetry has become increasingly more international, thus *more relevant to the human condition*, largely thanks to Robert Bly's leadership. He wants us to learn to share, to *transcend* our world & personal isolation, & to become responsible world citizens. Auden was wrong. Poetry *can* make something happen.

Hence This Cradle
by Hélène Sanguinetti
translated by Ann Cefola
(Otis Books/Seismicity Editions, Los Angeles, CA)

In *Hence This Cradle* (originally published in Paris, France as *Dísi, de ce berceau*, Flammarion, 2003), Hélène Sanguinetti blurs the distinctions between poetry & fiction with a breath-taking variety of different voices which ultimately cohere into a single universal persona that is simultaneously no one & everyone. The collection functions primarily as a long poem composed of fragments of "MESSAGES ADDRESSED, SLIPPED, LEFT BEHIND, ONLY THOUGHT, NEVER READ, LOST, MESSAGES PRESERVED WITH FEVER, FEVER-DENIED-TORN TO PIECES, ONE DAY ONCE AGAIN A FRESH LUMP BEATING IN THE THROAT."

The above fragment appears at the beginning of the book, almost like an extra set of alternative titles. Sanguinetti lets her inner dialogue flow. One gets the impression that her compositional process is based in spontaneity. She provides the reader with numerous minute particulars, images of smallness (a cricket, a snail, a fly, a pebble, a bee) contrasted with images of vastness, the "brilliant sea that breathes," the stars, the timelessness of love. Sanguinetti utilizes odd phraseology, syntax, blended nouns & other devices that serve to create a stuttering, disjointed effect. On the surface, this effect is a distinctly non-linear expression. A more careful reading reveals an emotional coherence that carries throughout. Translator Ann Cefola does a heroic job dealing with the challenge of translating from one of the most evocative & connotative languages in the world to one of the least, without reducing the already reductive & evasive language of the original into nonsense language. By working closely with Sanguinetti, Cefola has preserved the integrity of the piece remarkably well, with a few notable exceptions.

Not far into the book, an association to another great book that approached similar territory, (but from the fictional direction), asserted itself. This book also used a variety of voices to reveal a coherent persona at the end. It, like *Hence This Cradle*, also used different type styles to indicate shifts in point of view. The other book is *Steps*, which won Jerzy Kosinski the 1968 National Book Award. Both writers project their parts into their work, to see them integrated at the end of the book. Sanguinetti uses different typefaces & sizes, or all upper case or all lower case, to create the patchwork quilt of the poem. The 'heart' of the poem is actually printed in red ink - the only red ink in the book.

Ultimately, the poem becomes a symbol of the struggle of love in a world of chaos, death, light, laughter, tears - the whole gamut of human experience. Then, there is the recurrent evocation of mystery. Here are a few examples: *"It's the mystery of this loss that's important to me."* (pg. 53) *"Mystery of the lost Child, his Sandals / Mystery mule! / Mystery bonnet with small bells,"* (pg. 55) *"have you an answer to this mystery which makes one slip and / at the same time pushes with the horns' tip down to the sea and / it's sun, ice or even sky / or still night still more night, totally ignored?"* (pg. 81) *"In the garden, / I met a snail: I greeted him, / like a man. He too, too loaded with / mystery to be ignored."* (pg. 103)

Sanguinetti favors images that evoke the Mediterranean. (Cypress trees, volcanic Mount Vesuvius, seascapes.) She lived for a time at Arles, the countryside that inspired Van Gogh & Cèzanne. There are images of childhood juxtaposed with intimate notes between lovers, recurrent images of snails, approaching lava - all harmonically dissonant & ironic.

Finally, there is a recurrent reference to the mystery of death. Images of death, contrasted to images of life, recur throughout the poem:

> *Acrobat has such grace despite heavy*
> *thoughts*
> *in one hour will have caught fire, die*
> *asphyxiated.*
> *Two tigers will also have burned without a clue.*
> *Scents of great Africa,*
> *mysterious Asia lingering*
> *in their nostrils, oh! tigers, do not depart*
> *our earth!*
> (pg. 81)

Sanguinetti's readers are faced with either participating in the poem or being left out completely. Interestingly, the poem is potentially all-encompassing as a symbol of the positive & negative forces that both play on, & are played with by individuals caught in a given place & time. Many interpretations are possible with this kind of open-ended, yet cumulative type of literature. The reader is invited to explore the mystery of its meaning, as a *participant.*

Born in 1951, Sanguinetti is a member of the post-post-modern baby boom generation. As with most of that generation (myself included) the aesthetic value of the deconstruction of established forms & conventions is apparent. Translator Ann Cefola is generally sensitive to our generation's aesthetic post-post-modern sensibility in her choices of synonyms. There are a few places where she might have translated with more of a French accent. I believe that those aspects of the original that are universal, such as punctuation & line breaks, should be preserved intact. Because poetry allows for noun-verb inversions & highly personalized & idiosyncratic syntax, the inversions also can be preserved/translated, especially from Latin-based Romance languages such as French, Italian & Spanish. Also, some words, such as *chambre*/chamber could have been translated *as themselves*. While 'chamber' is a *bit* archaic in English, it's still much more evocative than 'bedroom.' (It evokes the many-chambered nautilus.) Changes in syntax are serious in poetry. They can damage the poetic process as it is perceived in a certain order by a reader. For the most part, though, Cefola succeeds in keeping the tone & imagery of the original, no small feat in a work that poses the question of how "to drift with the debris of the world and not drown?"

I like this book very much & recommend it to those who read poetry for experience. It is a sensual time-trip that expands from magnifying glass to telescope, transcending the boundaries of space.

They
by Spiel
(March Street Press, Greensboro, NC)

The poet Spiel develops personae of deep intensity. His work is confrontational & contains strong elements of drama. In *They*, Spiel expresses himself in the voice of a hypersensitive, perhaps autistic child, who is alienated from others, paranoid & frightened. I thought of Edgar Allan Poe's work, written from the point of view of a psychotic. (*The Tell-Tale Heart, The Raven*, etc.)

For most poets, such a voice would be an inauthentic conceit, but these pieces do have an authenticity that comes from Spiel's own childhood experiences. He has been open about his history of mental/emotional problems. There is ample autobiographical/inner detail here, but I'm not sure it goes all the way to the universal as poetry.

The publisher's note on the back cover states that "The bulk of this landmark Spiel collection was conveyed to the poet under the influence of an angry muse speaking in a convoluted tongue and set in raw exposure of the ubiquitous *theys* in our lives..."

Salvador Dali famously theorized that insanity, particularly paranoia, is a fertile source of artistic inspiration. As a leading surrealist, Dali described his own work as an expression of a paranoid state. The precedents in literature are numerous. It takes a special artist to transform it into authentic art.

Spiel's persona in this collection is pared down to raw fear, revealing an alienated soul without decoration. The tone is deliberately monotonous, yet histrionic. Spiel lets the reader in, but he doesn't accommodate us. He wants us to feel his pain. Spiel is often histrionic to a degree that his poems go over the top & seem contrived. Alan Catlin, in his introduction, aptly notes that no one writes quite like Spiel. Indeed, Spiel's style is a peculiar one, idiosyncratic & self-referential. It certainly illuminates some dark corners of the poets psyche, but it doesn't completely translate to the universal for me. The same criticism leveled at Sigmund Freud may be directed at Spiel - Freud's work was flawed by the fact that he only studied mentally-ill subjects to form his theories, without establishing a concept or study of normalcy first.

I'm not sure if the odd & inconsistent distortion of pronouns adds to the effect. In some cases the device adds another layer of meaning, but the disruption of mood serves little purpose other than to break the monotony,& is ultimately not poetically cost effective. Spiel's work is uneven for me. Often I find it dramatic & thought-provoking, but other times I feel that it's self-indulgent. Heavy use of epigrams on nearly every poem is a bit off-putting, because the quotes do not relate directly to the poems they introduce, & they break the mood.

This poetry is too emotionally raw for mere enjoyment. Spiel reveals the obsessive nature of fear & paranoia, but it's a hard-sell unless you've been through it. Spiel asserts that there are those who suffer in ways most of us simply can't see. This is the book's primary value. The poet functions as a voice for the doomed.

Certainly even paranoids have real enemies, but *they* don't distinguish between enemies & friends. There are no friends in this book, nor are there solutions. Just angst, & plenty of it, Kafkaesque & unrelenting.

Spiel is an acquired taste, but he does push the envelope of poetry to the edge of drama. The mental illness aspect of his work is both intriguing & frustrating. One is tempted to ask what this gifted artist would have done had he not been a victim of mental illness, but it's not really a fair question. His work has value just as it is, but a large audience will probably elude him. Nothing new about that in the avant-garde.

Inrue & *Outside The End*
by Guy Beining
(Phrygian Press, Bayside, NY)
(The Silver Wonder Press, Chicago, IL,)

Inrue

Guy Beining gets into words & their ambiguities like few other poets. Though driven primarily by concept, Beining transcends the purely intellectual. He manages, somehow, to put himself in his works, despite their consistent structural & other controls, relative to the concept being explored. His poems make non-linear sense. Or, he can be read as an abstract lyricist whose poetry is driven by word association & imagination. Either way, I always find it intriguing. Mystery is one source of intrigue in Beining's work. The references are often obscure & idiosyncratic, but they are intriguing to a reader who can suspend disbelief - a prerequisite in most art & literature. Many of the poems are in past tense, & contain small stories & observations. Beining pushes the envelope of content & structure, & expresses himself in a unique, flexible style.

* * *

Outside The End

This chapbook collects eleven poems & seven artworks by the highly idiosyncratic multi-media artist/poet Guy Beining. Beining's poems are well-illustrated by his collages & ink drawings, in that both achieve a similar ambiguous mixture of images. Seemingly disparate images imply deeper meaning when combined in the same work. This is equally true of both graphic & poetic art. The first four poems were written between 5/7/01 & 5/9/01, & bear their dates & the title *almost complete*. These poems attempt to approach the ineffable.

They each fall short, intentionally or unintentionally, & are thus 'almost complete.' The rest of the poems reveal a Zen ambivalence: "when you can fall thru earth/you finally begin to realize that/there is nothing there/ & for that you have spent a lifetime writing." My favorite poem is *copy the water XLVI*. Beining keeps my attention.

The Ristorante Godot & Wedlock Sunday and Other Poems

by Gerald Locklin

(Bottle of Smoke Press, Dover, DE)
(Liquid Paper Press, Austin, TX)

In **The Ristorante Godot** Gerald Locklin achieves a nice balance between his ekphrasic poems & his poems of personal revelation. In the moving poem *the gift of life*, Locklin uses his perfectly vernacular language to meld the personal revelation & the meditative ekphrasic poems into one evocative & poignant poem. Casually profound, the poem goes much deeper than its surface would imply. Locklin is a confessor, & an honest one. He's also a pleasurable poet, who feels an obligation to entertain to a large degree. I think he can do this because he loves art & language & the many forms they take. Many of the poems in this slim collection are 'about' how aging changes ones perspective. Locklin is a personality poet, & the apparent easiness of his work should not be mistaken for superficiality. He deals with big issues in an ironically casual way. A neatly produced, well-edited collection of poems that will bear repeated readings.

* * *

Wedlock Sunday and Other Poems contains several substantial poems by the prolific topical poet Gerald Locklin. The personal revelation poems, such as the title poem, *Enough Is All You Need*, & *Guides*, are the more emotionally evocative. The ekphrasic poems fall into two patterns: those about the paintings & those originally inspired by paintings, that exploded projectively as a form of Rorschach. In the latter category, Locklin taps the original source or artistic impulse of the painter whose painting is another, parallel work stemming from the same

61

source, out of the ether. In some, like *Currier & Ives: The Four Seasons*, he does both, going one step beyond the original in the final section, to contrast our present day experience to a simpler time. Every aesthetic & life experience is of topical value to this poet who wants to penetrate to essential truths, for he sees constantly.

Think & London Nov 6-Nov 11
by Mark Sonnenfeld
(Marymark Press, East Windsor, NJ)

Think

Now for something completely different! Mark Sonnenfeld is achieving levels of poetic insight that may only be reached through a complete disarrangement of the senses. (As recommended by Rimbaud.) In *Think,* Sonnenfeld transcends his cut-up experiments but does not leave their flexibility & freshness behind. His new word-collages go beyond the subjective experience of the poet to present the reader with many unequivocally original arrangements. The organizing mind of the wildly divergent poet is everywhere in evidence, in a good way. One can see the value of his previous experiments in Sonnenfeld's latest voice. This chapbook has an almost magical coherence. These are not throwaways, though they are difficult & often non-linear. They live up to the title, & ask the reader to *be* the poet, & *think.* Highly recommended for those who want to see the boundaries of language & association. Some of Sonnenfeld's best work ever.

* * *

London Nov 6 - Nov 11

Sonnenfeld captures the feeling of an American in London in this small collection of photos & short poems. He is a true artist, whose personal vision is deeply deconstructionist. Meaning emerges like steam escaping from a hole in a pipe. Sonnenfeld knows it when he sees it. He is primarily known for his poetry collages, & cut-up work, but his talents go far beyond that conception. He also has a great photographic eye. One photo, of 5 Abbey Road, has the graffiti message *What is art?* This chapbook goes well with Mark's photo collection of the NYC subway, in which he uses photo-images of trash to reveal the stories of those who littered it. The poem(s) also work together as a single poem. Read separately, they are deconstructed haiku. Sonnenfeld is a primitive genius. He challenges the readers, poetic convention, & above all, himself.

Summer With All Its Clothes Off
by Art Beck
(Gravida, New York, NY)

This slim, attractively produced selection of stunning poems by Art Beck is a great pleasure. Beck has a keen lyrical sense as well as a painterly eye for visual imagery. The poems are introspective, yet evocative. The tone varies from pensive to poignant to playful, putting the poet's personality at the center of it all. The passage of time, seen in moments, & longing, are Beck's major themes in this collection. Each poem has its own special feeling, driven by Beck's lyrical melodies & harmonics. My personal favorites are *To Annie from the Winter Coast, Cottage* & *Here it is, Memorial Day at Clear Lake again,*. The tasteful letterpress production of the collection suits the contents. Editor Lynne Savitt's selection is sensitive & skillful.

Living Proof
by **Mary Bonina**
(Červená Barva Press, Somerville, MA)

Mary Bonina has a light touch with a narrative. Her poems are easy to follow & she knows when she has told us enough. Her endings are succinct & leave us with a final insight culminating from deft images that precede it. In poems like *The Big Questions* & *Boy, 5*, Bonina contemplates her son's perception & nicely evokes the intellectual & experiential gap between parents & children that is only bridged through love. Indeed, children & their changes is a major subject for Mary Bonina. She writes as a mother/poet, & her compassion & sense of wonder is revealed in every poem. Her language is natural & her poems scan. They are polished without seeming ornamental or contrived. She has a developed voice, comfortable & direct. She is an observer of nature, children, self. "Funny,/how truth will come to you sometimes when/you least expect it, when all you are thinking about is/what you'll have for dinner and the nice grape tart for dessert." Another fine Červená Barva book.

Still Life
by Alan Catlin
(Black Buzzard Press, Austin, TX)

      Alan Catlin paints elegiac poetic still life(s) in his descriptively detailed run-on style in *Still Life*. Catlin has a painter's eye, keen for details. Description is his forte, mixed with a dash of subtle irony. He is objectivistic, in that he allows his images to speak for themselves. He is an astute people-watcher, & a poet/reporter. His intense interest in human character feeds his prolific output a legion of subjects. Catlin paints a wide variety of dead & dying 'still life(s)' - elderly nursing home inmates, a punk rockette, the ghosts of Gettysburg, a dead baseball player, crash victims & other fatalities, all presented in a subtly foreboding, elegiac tone. Death scenes are repeatedly rendered into neutral by the poet's detachment. They who were once so alive are inexorably gone. My personal favorites are the ones that picture the fey, like *Jim Carroll and Friends Performing at J.B. Scott's,* & *Black and White Punk Rockette on the Schenectady to Albany Bus, 1984.* A strong, relentless collection by one of our master poets.

Among Us
by Harris Gardner
(Červená Barva Press, Somerville, MA)

Harris Gardner dares to tackle philosophical issues, achieving a spiritual level lesser poets shouldn't attempt. His style is an impressive mixture of lyricism, tongue-in-cheek humor & simultaneously serious philosophical dialogue that engages & compels us along a surreal narrative line, with iconic angelic players. I am reminded of *The Screwtape Letters* by C.S. Lewis. Both writers use artistic parables, & are masters of multi-leveled symbolism. Both use biblical metaphors to address moral issues. Gardner is more Old Testament than Lewis, however. On one level, the poems explore the classic conflict of man's spirituality versus his baser impulses. The morality of writing poetry itself is another major theme. Gardner achieves an elevated formal language at points. His poetic ear is impeccable, & his use of lyrical devices is subtle & effective. A sublime tour de force by a uniquely talented poet.

Illegal Border Crosser
by Michael Graves
(Červená Barva Press, Somerville, MA)

Michael Graves writes with clarity & in an easy vernacular, but his content often features figures from classical mythology. It's an intelligent mix, because the accessible language helps us swallow the classical references better than a more formal approach would with the same content. Classical allusions are problematic in poetry, because they seem contrived, impersonal & academic. His best poems address relationships & how to express love across barriers of time, ego & space. His easy language works perfectly in poems like *Mother* & *No Cover Girl.* The title poem *Illegal Border Crosser* is an evocative piece of writing that reveals a Whitmanic poet's soul. Graves identifies with the same leaves of grass as Whitman: "I love the empty neighborhoods of night/the buzzing thrumming city/when it slows/and skeleton crews/and revelers or solitary citizens/possess the streets." Michael Graves is a poet of universal vision.

Vanishing Points
by Gayle Elen Harvey
(The Sow's Ear Poetry Review, Milkwood, VA)

Gayle Elen Harvey is a sensuous poet whose poems are highly visual. Her major theme is the distance between people, & emotional 'vanishings.' Her imagery carries the poems along through the mental movies she generates for the reader to visualize. *Fishing Lock 18, Late Summer* is a good example of Harvey's visual association & also of her ease with extended metaphor. In other works, she skillfully interweaves erotic & spiritual images. Sensuality permeates her poems, regardless of subject. Another constant is her use of irony, always a mark of poetic depth. Moonlight illuminates many of her poems, a metaphor for wonder & magic. From *Art Student*: "Seeing/is deliberate as moonlight. Something knife-edged. Fallen/into." See also *Woman and Bird in Moonlight*, one of her best poems, inspired by the painting by Miro. Many of her poems are ekphrasic, drawing inspiration from visual artworks. Gayle Elen Harvey is a talented poet whose work penetrates beyond surfaces to deeper levels, in search of connections.

Blue Ribbons At The County Fair
by Ellaraine Lockie
(PWJ Publishing, Tehama, CA)

Her poetry is rich in imagery. Her poems scan & are often based in sophisticated syllabic cadences. She often projects a naive, rural persona, yet exhibits the poetic gifts of a master. She can portray a wise older woman, an emotionally driven young woman, a participatory reporter or social commentator. She is a craftswoman with a message, whose poems capture her responses to the memories & stories that form the backbone of her work. There is a confessional aspect to her work. She is a poet of personal honesty who is unashamed to share her insights & perceptions & let the chips fall as they may. Every poem in this collection shines. They have all won contests & awards, after all. This 'editing' has resulted in a high quality 'selected poems' without being called that. Ellaraine is a true independent, unphased by literary convention. Above all, I am always impressed with her confident natural wisdom, as revealed in poems like *Autumn's End, Imperfection Ears Closed, Eyes Open, The Affair*. She is one of the best, & *Blue Ribbons At The County Fair* is essential Lockie, worth twice the price.

The Alchemy Of Words
by Edward Francisco
(Birch Brook Press, Delhi, NY)

Edward Francisco delves into the abstract meaning of words in search of passageways to deeper levels of meaning. His grounding in Zen is everywhere apparent, & there are some precious Zen gems here, such as *Chu Hsi, Logos, Alchemy* & *The Way*.

Here are some lines from **The Way**:

"The more a man progresses
on the Way,
the more his feeling of being
a stranger intensifies.
Soon he becomes boring.
Later still, unbearable.
Finally, odious."

(page 19)

Francisco uses abstract words in the way an imagist uses images; he opens mysterious doors for the reader to enter blindly, feeling around for the light-switch. His poems evoke the paradoxes of life & language, exploring the fine nuances, searching for the magical formula of revelation. Francisco engages the reader by inviting him to join the brotherhood of alchemists. About 25% of his poems end with a question. I love this approach. It makes me want to re-read them. His emphasis on paradox is a refreshing departure from most abstract writing. His poems demonstrate how abstract words can be suited to poetry, the essence of which is the revelation of the great mysteries of life. As a bonus, this collection is beautifully printed on vellum via letterpress. For those familiar with Birch Brook Press, this is no surprise. For those who aren't, the Birch Brook experience would be like tasting a fine wine for the first time, wondering how you could have missed it up to now. Francisco writes with intelligence & insight about the unseen world that exists beneath the surface.

The Republic Of Lies
by Ed Ochester
(Adastra Press, Easthampton, MA)

In another beautifully printed, limited edition from Gary Metras' Adastra Press, Ed Ochester presents us with a deceptively colloquial collection. Ochester is a master of subtlety, with a great ear. His conversational style creates a tension with the ultimately serious subjects & ideas of his poems. In this small collection of poems, he uses topical references to evoke the universal, & he does it with what appears at first glance to be great ease. Upon further examination, the poems are skillfully & subtly constructed.

His work has an irony that I admire. He is socially observant & critical. The first poem *September, Listening To The Old Songs* is a memorable evocation of Zen awareness versus sad nostalgia. The title poem, *The Republic Of Lies*, exploits his sense of irony to the max, exposing the hypocrisy that is the main theme of the collection. Each poem contributes to the vision of American society as illusory & hypocritical, a 'republic of lies.' Ochester examines social values through parable, & anecdote.

From ***The Republic Of Lies****:*

Hitler could be generous.
Imagine that. He was
furious, but did nothing
other than remove Baldur
from his trust forever.
Can you imagine talking
to power that way?
For the deaths
of a few nameless
women and girls?

What good would it do?
What was she thinking?   (page 10)

This edition is limited to 326 copies. You'd be lucky to get one, at twice the price.

Ten Songs From Bulgaria
by Linda Nemec Foster
(Červená Barva Press, Somerville, MA)

This sensitively written suite of short poems transcends the merely ekphrasic, though the poems are based in the photographs of Jacko Vassilev. The real test of an ekphrasic work is its ability to stand alone as an autonomous work. Linda Nemec Foster proves that the *how* out-trumps the *what*. Her poems are evocative & life-affirming, despite the images of loss, fear & smallness.

She also reveals her sensibility in the natural but distinct form of each poem. Taken together, they transcend beyond the sum of their parts. Linda Nemec Foster writes highly condensed poetry that expands upon contemplation. Subtle lyricism combines in her work with moral depth. These are gems: *Cry of Freedom, The Dancing Bear, Child With Dove, A Man is a Man When a Man is on the Road.* In *The Dancing Bear*, the transcendent quality is perfectly illustrated. Reprinted in full:

The Dancing Bear

Once upon a time, I did not exist
in this frozen pose. Only danced
in your dreams like a myth:
bear of elegant waltz and measured
fox-trot; bear of passionate tango
and manic jitterbug. Now look at me.
Reduced to a muzzle and chain, serenaded
by a fool with a clumsy violin. I refuse
to dance, cannot remember the basic steps.
Music of the forest stuck in my throat.

(page 16)

Linda Nemec Foster has presented us with an

elegant suite of poems, concise but profound in their moral depth.

Light At The End - The Jesus Poems
by Lyn Lifshin
(Clevis Hook Press, Rochester, N Y)

No one can milk a metaphor like Lyn Lifshin. Her new collection is a tour de force & an instant classic. She dares to work with emotionally & historically laden public symbols in her work, thus challenging the prevailing poetic values. She's done Barbie, Marilyn Monroe & Madonna as ongoing symbols of femininity in previous collections. These new poems, subtitled *The Jesus Poems,* plumb new depths & reach new heights of insight.

These are not Christian or religious poems. In fact, the literally minded might find them blasphemous. Jesus is used as a metaphor, in a wide variety of ways. Ultimately, she uses icons for their symbolism, in the way that Robert Mapplethorpe has done in visual art. Hopefully, her reception will be better than Mapplethorpe's.

These poems are rich with metaphor & association. Lifshin is unyielding in her drive to deep dive. Taken as a group, their complexity & virtuosity are truly unprecedented in contemporary poetry. She puts so much skill & feeling into each poem that they cannot easily be reduced to their elements. When she wants to be simple, she can be, but when she digs deeply, the result is multi-leveled, evocative & universal. On the immediate level her subject is mankind's yearning for a savior. On a deeper level, Lifshin expresses the feminine nature of that yearning.

The poems were composed a few years ago for an anthology Denise Duhamel was doing. A much smaller version was brought out by the small press Future Tense & was a quick sell out. This larger book, beautifully & lavishly illustrated by photographer-artist Lindsay Herko, was developed by Clevis Hook Press after they saw some of the unpublished poems through a submission to their magazine *HazMat Review*.

This much-expanded version gets the complete Lifshin treatment, & is astonishing in its range. There are psychosexual levels mixed with cultural iconography & religious/spiritual levels & she puts enough of herself into it to succeed on that ongoing level as well. Her deep intelligence & poetic sensibility are everywhere apparent. No single example or quotation illustrates all of this. The parts add up to a much greater total in Lifshin's brave, intense work. Here's a snippet I like for its deft imagery:

"We gathered violets as the sun went / down, soaked them overnight in the blue bowl and mixed / them with pectin and paraffin until the violet jelly glowed / amethyst in a jar near a window until snow when he rushed /out, as if the stars were in the yard, gathering the / flakes, holding them up to me like fine crystals or / lace from the angels fluttering above our heads as he was / over me, bringing berries and cream up to the garnet room / before spreading himself over me like those stars"

(from *Jesus And The Garden*)

Lyn Lifshin is a poetic virtuoso. Much has been said about her prolific output, but the truly phenomenal aspect of her poetry is its consistent high quality & depth. *Light At The End* once again confirms her status as a major poet of the boom generation.

Something Is Burning In Brooklyn
by Linda Lerner
(Iniquity Press/Vendetta Books, Manasquan, NJ)

Linda Lerner is a poet who bravely articulates the emotions of fear & loss on both a personal & universal level. Her latest chapbook continues in the vein of *City Woman* (2006) & *Living In Dangerous Times* (2007), making art out of anxiety, ultimately finding redemption within oneself. Lerner is a poet of social protest & existential angst, but ultimately she finds strength to go on in the human capacity for love. This is the unifying element in her work that gives it universal appeal. She reaches to express the ineffable, contrasting the dark & light sides of human nature. The conflict between the alienation of a big anonymous city & the need of the individual for meaningful experience provides the tension in her work. This is reinforced by a language that hovers on the edge of articulation, reaching for the right words. In the title poem she gets in the groove:

> "nothing and no time to squeeze but
> another sour tasting second
> hungry for something sweet and
> worn out looking for the fire"

Her m/o is New York colloquial with a hipster edge. The city images are precise & crisp, reflecting a keen perception. From *Driving America*:

> "two women in jeans, stiletto heels
> rings in their noses, lips,
> *bring the troops home* buttons on
> jackets point to the car,

"it rocks" one shouts, he looks out,
abruptly rear ended by 2008;
"hey mister," the woman cries,
"if you're going to Williamsburg,
can you give us a lift?"

Linda Lerner's work ranges from gritty to the edge of
sentimental, occupying the linguistic borderland between
Street & Beat with a tough but feminine sensibility. She
evokes the struggle of human dignity & determination in
the face of a depersonalizing urban environment. Hers is
a fire with plenty of fuel to burn.

Nothing Divine Here
by Gloria Mindock
(Ušokuštampa, Cetinje and Montenegro & Springfield, VA)

Gloria Mindock's new collection burns with the blue intensity of gasoline. Mindock shines a revealing light into the darkest corners of emotion. Her voices echo against our mental walls & penetrates deeply into the heart of darkness. But, where Joseph Conrad advises us to "kill them all," Mindock would have us *feel* them all.

In her author's note Mindock tells us that "This book is only an accumulation of all the stories I heard written in first person." When I asked her about her identification with the personae in the poems, she reiterated that "None of the poems are about me but written in first person... I decided to write in first person like I was the one going through all this stuff. Being a social worker helps me with empathy... It seems like I write all my poems in first person. It sounds more personal that way. I wanted to connect with the readers."

As a former social worker myself, I understand. She wanted to connect with the people whose stories she tells. A social worker cannot afford to be too professionally detached. It's *ineffective.* But, over-identifying with people in trouble can put you on the emotional roller coaster with them. It's a precarious balance. These poems represent that balance. They are how Mindock as a poet/social worker, both integrates & synthesizes her experiences into poems both sympathetic & universal.

She's immensely intelligent & courageous in her approach to poetry. There is a primal depth to these poems. Her use of organic imagery is unique & contributes to the overall theme of integration between persons, persons with themselves & ultimately persons with spiritual beings. She has been influenced by Rilke, & the influence is never more apparent than in her conversations with angels:

> "In the absence of love, the trees,
> embraced my pain. They are my keepsake.
> Oh Angel, hear my thoughts...love me.
> If you can't, reach in for my heart, and remove
> it with pliers. Fling it up into the air.
> I will taste your power and be
> registered in life as a singing
> bird hating seeds."
>
> (from *My Siege)*

  Her multi-voiced approach yields a level of drama that evokes for me the function of the Greek chorus in Sophocles or the diversity of Edgar Lee Masters' *Spoon River Anthology.* The tone that bridges the gaps & unifies these poems is the overriding persona of their author. Through her control of both tone & diction, Mindock infuses her work with universality.

  The tone is set by the first poem, *Water,* which stands alone before the six divided sections of the book, to signify its universality. Here's the first stanza:

> "I realized one thing
> about my life today
> It doesn't matter
> years from now
> the company I had, will
> have ceased
> This planet will stop
> This universe
> exiled"

By placing these words at the beginning of her collection, she ties all the voices that follow into one that flows like water, a symbol for earthly life. The modern existential dilemma is poetically evoked through her use of universal symbolism. The poet's voice is colloquial enough to avoid the usual over-elegance associated with heavy symbolism.

In the middle (4th) section, in a sequential poem *Doppelganger*, she explores how we both reflect & conflict with an "other" within ourselves. *Doppelganger* is a major work which can't be dealt with adequately here. I have been transported by it each time I've read it. The language & imagery are nothing short of exquisite. She channels Rilke or taps into the same well in this one. *Doppelganger* is worth the price of the book by itself.

Gloria Mindock magically transmutates experience into her poems with an intensity that is rare even among poets. Despite its focus on the existential, the impenetrable & the ineffable, these poems are full of life, if not life-affirming. They have the heat of a deep burn branded into the pages.

After Shakespeare: Selected Sonnets
by George Held
(Červená Barva Press, Somerville, MA)

George Held's new collection is an appealing balance of form and content that uses classical sonnet techniques and strophes to present an intimate portrait of its author. Stepping outside current trend, Held is determined to stay true to himself without concern for parochial prohibitions against rhyme and meter, and abstraction. The poetic pleasure comes from two sources: Held's verbal skill (witty, lyrical) and his honesty in showing us his feelings, attitudes and fears.

Death is one of the major strophes of the collection. As a fellow poet in his mid-sixties, I understand the fascination. Such awareness is hard won.

Although he displays a significant formalist orientation, he avoids the pitfall that the less skillful formalists fall into, which is the elevation of form over function. (i.e. Syntactical inversions to achieve clunky end-rhymes.)

In a way, Held parodies classic sonnet conventions. In another sense he simply pushes the envelope of the sonnet form, integrating the English, Petrarchian, etc. styles into what might best be termed hyper sonnets or better, hybrid sonnets. Rather than deconstruct and paste, as Ted Berrigan did in his famous *The Sonnets*, Held builds on past tradition while adding a modern consciousness and language. He expands traditional sonnet values into a synthesis of new and old. In this sense, he is working in the area I call *Transmutational Forms*. These are personalized treatments of received forms, such as haiku that do not conform to either the seasonal reference 'rule' or even the syllabics, but still capture the *essence* of that enduring form.

Another example can be seen in the many transmutations of the ancient Persian ghazal, such as in the ghazals of Jim Harrison or in my own.

The collection is divided into four sections. The short first section contains four poems that define the themes that follow in the succeeding three. The first poem addresses the book's title, *After Shakespeare*, which is both a serious consideration of the very endeavor of writing anything in the face of the complex history of man and planet, while simultaneously batting a facetious wink at us with his tongue in his cheek. He addresses his doubts head-on at the beginning. We realize upon entry that the poems will be multi-leveled, thoughtful, and crafted. The first poem sets the tone:

After Shakespeare

When suicides exceed the rate of birth,
And survivors doubt the worth of living;
When signs of hope have vanished from the earth,
And altruists have given up on giving;
When "quality of life" has lost its spark,
And euthanists no longer cast a pall;
When wildlife can't expect another Ark,
And mankind claws for its own survival;
Will anyone write or read a sonnet?
Will time at last have undone Shakespeare's line,
As with marble and gilded monuments,
Since lost will be all sense of the sublime?
If so, how vain of sonneteers to think
Their lines will last as life becomes extinct.

The second and third sections of the book are the most personal, composed of elegies and philosophical meditations on mortality. My favorite of the elegies is *How Dad Died*. Here are the last three lines: "Dad had died of a self-inflicted wound, / leaving me beyond suspicion but with / a red vision that makes me catch my breath." One may see from these lines that classical form and resolution serves George Held's vision and self expression. He's made it his own, though his vision is ultimately existential-humanist.

Of the meditations, my personal favorite from the second section is *New Fears*. Here's the Wordsworthian first line: "When I have fears that we shall cease to be,".

The middle section, *Apostrophes*, contains twenty-one poems 'To' Moon, Anger, Depression, Cupidity, Boredom, Reason, Nostalgia, etc. Through ideas and feelings, these poems portray their author with subtle but distinct precision.

In the final section, the last poem is the most personal and moving in the book. It serves as a conclusion to all the doubts, fears and grim realities of the preceding poems:

Finding My Way
For CFH

What does it mean to "find my way" at sixty-two - that the path's grown clearer, or my focus?
Who gets the credit - me, my shrink, or you?
Do I cheer or lament the years I've lost - that I was no DiMaggio or Bill Gates, no Yeats, but one with time and words to waste, an ex-Beatnik, ex-Hippie, at what cost?
But past's not prologue; now I take my ease, content to be wakened by Euterpe's call or caressed to ecstasy by you, who prescribe more play and lots less labor: aging Sybarites, we indulge anew, annihilating all thought death's in store.
Have I found my way by following you?

Knowing oneself is the key to finding a way. The way originates in self-knowledge but expands beyond the self. Held poses it as both a profound philosophical question and a deeply personal one in the last line of *Finding My Way.*

After Shakespeare - Selected Sonnets is a refreshing collection from a serious talent, intelligent and engaging. A multi-leveled masterpiece that proves that good poetry may flourish outside current notions of poetical correctness.

A Very Funny Fellow
by Donald Lev
(NYQ Books, New York, NY)

Donald Lev writes poems that are deceptively simple yet infused with a subtle irony that gives them a poignant intimacy. He achieves this through his reliance on directness and honesty. The word that comes to mind for me is *persona*. Lev is from that school of poets whom Frank O'Hara called personists. Poets like Lyn Lifshin, John Bennett, the late Hugh Fox and the later Charles Bukowski have tried to use their real selves as the persona in all their poems. They're attempting to pin themselves down, to achieve self-understanding through their poems. It isn't that they're explaining themselves. No, it's more than that. It's an attempt at real communication through *honesty.*

This kind of poetry is akin to confessional poetry, but it's not so precious or constricted, so restricted to a gothic mood. Thus, the title: *A Very Funny Fellow.* It's mostly ironic, but there is a subtle level of Zenlike humor in Lev's acceptance of himself and his own foibles and weaknesses.

Lev makes a good Everyman. He arrives on feet of clay to consider the big metaphysical questions. We all must, however ill-equipped we are for ultimate success. The poems bear a resemblance to ancient Chinese poets such as Li Po, who wrote "When I'm drunk, I lose Heaven and Earth. / Frozen - I stick to my lonely bed. / At last I forget that I exist, / And then my joy is truly great." (My translation.)

It's a subtle type of humor that relies on deep irony. All humor relies on irony, but it's the depth and humility that matter here. A few examples should help:

"Exile is fantasy. The past never was.

All that ever was for me is here,
sitting in my chair, seeking images."
                     from *When I Seek An Image*

"Drunks are always meditating
on the protective shell around them.
How brittle it is."
                     from *Drunks*

Lev also goes beyond the aphoristic quality of the above quotes to poems of more obvious ironic humor, such as *Sin*, quoted here in full:

Sin

There was this rule:
thou shalt not piss
upon the Tree of Life.
But I had to go.
The next gas station
wouldn't be for another
thirty-five miles and I
just couldn't hold it any longer.
So I pulled off the road and
went behind this tree.
How could I have known
it was that tree. And I
never heard of that particular
rule. Maybe I wasn't listening or
something. I shouldn't feel guilty,
should I? Should I?
The Tree of Life just shriveled
up and died. How could I have known?
                     Sin, pg 84

Although they appear easy and colloquial, poems like these are actually finely tuned little machines. The best artists always make it look easy. These utterances come from age and experience and from terrible loss. Less can be more when it comes to sentimentality, yet Lev communicates the intensity of his feelings simply and elegantly:

Lines In Winter
for Enid

Snowflakes cling to the yew hedge
furnished by a cemetery's
program for perpetual care.

Many miles away I watch
snow gather
upon denuded rose of sharon bushes
outside my window.

A shadow
passed behind me
just now. I felt it.

Something's vanished.
Nothing has taken its place.

Lines In Winter, pg 68

For Donald Lev, the writing *is* easy, compared to all the living that led to it. Yet we get the impression, that his writing is also *essential* to his ongoing sanity, and this is the redemption of poetry itself in the hands of a master.

The Devil's Sonata
by David Chorlton
(Future Cycle Press, Lexington, KY)

David Chorlton's new book has an organic feeling to it, perhaps because Chorlton is a master of descriptive verse. He owes a debt to both the imagists and the objectivists. (Of course, those two movements were aesthetically related. There is little significant difference between relying strictly on imagery to produce a poetic response in the reader, or "no ideas except in things." Were Amy Lowell and Hilda Doolittle so different from Williams Carlos Williams or Charles Reznikoff?) Be that as it may, suffice it to say that as a poet, David Chorlton uses imagery and personal music to evoke reader response as his primary method. His content is familiar and loved territory to me, as I often choose to do the same thing. That is, contrast the ways of man to the ways of nature. Chorlton is a great observer of his environment as a descriptive poet must and should be. And the images do consistently evoke a particular feeling for me. There is a point in life when one settles into acceptance, and this alone can more than double a person's attention to external details and also to their intrinsic meanings. ('Ideas in things.') Chorlton is old enough, skilled enough and wise enough to be there. He's *solid*, and he can sing.

The poem *Birds from the Interstate* illustrates his keen observation and images. The images of the birds are positioned beside the affairs of men. The imagery provides the contrast as well as the feeling of zen acceptance:

Birds from the Interstate

Amid the sparse mesquite
all that moves

is a roadrunner
as he darts a stretch
then stops and darts again,
chasing the heat in a circle.
There's a brown-speckled breeze
in his feathers,
and his crest
points straight at the sun.

A freight train hauls a new shipment
from China past a flat
expanse of desert, where cracks
have risen to the surface
and the saguaros are riddled
with gunshot and drought.
They lean left and right
but grip the earth as gently
as white-winged doves grip them

when they perch at the tip
overlooking the land
on which billboards begin
by selling bets
as dice roll away from the road
in a casino cut
from raw chance and artificial lights,

then progress from
Marine recruiting
to redemption
to offering deals
that flash past too quickly
to read, while the ravens
who circle above them
want nothing
except the air and a place
to rest and caw black folly

at everything beneath them.

It is a type of 'desert music' that he provides us with in *The Devil's Sonata*. Despite his emphasis on imagery to evoke an intrinsic meaning, Chorlton actually presents us with a strong but subtle social commentary, which a reader perceives in the cumulative symbolism of the whole. Imagism and symbolism are very close in his work. When an image (such as birds) is recurrent in a poet's work, it crosses over into symbolism, if not public, then at least a private symbolism. It is in the nature of symbols that they are universal. For Chorlton, man's nature is over-shadowed by nature itself, and he wants us to know that. It's not *foreboding*, it's just true. The poet accepts it in a Zen-like way. But, he *sees* it, and reports it.

Not that this poetry is detached, however, but rather that it puts the feelings of the poet in the choice of images and the tone. It's subtle.

Chorlton more than meets my criteria for inclusion in the canon of the best poets of the Boom Generation. His lyricism is subtle and in a lower key, appropriate to the wisdom of his content. Satisfaction comes not from verbal excitement in his work, but rather it emanates from clear, lyrical use of imagery.

If you don't have a Chorlton book in your collection, *The Devil's Sonata* would be a great book to start with. One of our best, most solid poets, David Chorlton sings his desert music right into the heart.

Drastic Dislocations - New And Selected Poems
by Barry Wallenstein
(NYQ Books, New York, NY)

      Barry Wallenstein in *Drastic Dislocations* offers poetry readers a collection of uniquely musically-driven poems that are strikingly fresh and original. Although many or most of the poems are written to accompany or be accompanied by a small jazz combo, they have a music of their own which is clearly audible on the written page. I'm sure it would add a special level of experience to hear them read aloud, with or without accompaniment. It always does. But, unlike many performance pieces that lose too much when printed, Wallenstein's poems are also independent literary structures that succeed on purely literary values as well as being highly compatible with musical accompaniment.

      Here's an example:

In The Parlance of Mezz
after Mezz Mezznow

As Mezz used to say when tired—
after playing too excitedly for hours
and after hours and then topping it off
with too much good down brew; muggles too—
it's time "to stash my frame
between a deuce of lilywhites,"
and if that hurts the rhythm of my day
or alters the moves of some,
that's OK; after all, days do have their jaggeds.

"Plant you now and dig you later,"
is a farewell in spades I've said

and no offense;
I was born in the light of a stairwell
and have always been color-blind
or partial to black velvet day or night.
That's just my mind.

For some—me too for a patch of years—
it's been Weep City just around every turn
and the conveyance an express.
I'm off it now and sit miles from the station.
My misery's been gone for more than
a couple of chimes and I'm up sometimes
and playing quicker than a spinning dime.

I've known meanness too and stridency
and blades in the hands of tigers
hiding their purrs within.
I said one time to a cat with a permanent frown,
"You can afford the luxury of being a little delicate,
my friend." Fur bristled—gained his face a grin.

After all the times inside cells and cellblocks
and blocked in my own self too, I'm out and
in the music again. Pops is my guiding star
and it's all for the telling:
I'm a "skin full of contentment,
a bundle of happiness in a blue serge suit."

Musical poems attempt primarily to create a mood.
When the ideas in a poem go beyond mood producing
images, they produce or reveal an attitude in addition to
the musical mood. Jazz, blues and rock are all big on mood
and attitude. Barry Wallenstein's poetry is in a similar
groove.

In The Parlance Of Mezz illustrates Wallenstein's
use of the language of jazz. It's especially effective in the
double-entendre use of "I said one time to a cat with a

permanent frown," after establishing both sides of the metaphor skillfully. The original 'cat' is Mezz himself, and then by extension in the second stanza the poet. Cool cats. But then, in the fourth stanza just before the line in question, he establishes a tiger, but the overall metaphor continues. Then, "I said that one time to a cat..." Cages come next, themselves a metaphor for holding in ones own music. Music here, of course, is also used symbolically. There is no lack of depth or music in Barry Wallenstein's poems.

The major theme that runs through the collection is temporary salvation achieved through the discovery of ones own personal music and how it harmonizes with the sounds/music of the temporal world. In other, more concise words, *it's blues*. From *Distant Music*:

> The music heard faintly a week ago—/was it a horn or a voice/filtering through the woods—has stopped./Instead there is a metallic noise,/a sound of a sledge striking an anvil./Over the hill wood is scraping against itself;/there's that churning again and the siren.

It amuses the Muses to hear the poets sing their songs, each in a unique voice. Wallenstein contributes something special to our current chorus.

Relics Of Lust: New & Selected Poems

by Lynne Savitt

(NYQ Books, New York, NY)

In the hands of a lesser poet, the subjects of these poems could be in bad taste. However, in the case of natural poet Lynne Savitt, they simply taste good. Although sex is her primary metaphor for a life of passion, her true subject is her own conflict between the polarities of freedom and duty. Her personal struggles are transmuted into artistic tension in her poems, infusing them with a compelling vitality.

Savitt uses several limited poetic devices to impart a breathless quality into her poems. One of the most effective is her repeated use of the mid-line enjambment. I have not seen this used by anyone as often or usefully as Lynne. I asked her if she invented or inherited it, and her reply was that she 'just heard it that way.' Simply put, she uses one word to end an association and begin another one. When combined with her customary end-line enjambment, the poems rush breathlessly along. Her explanation: "I think it moves the poem along and sometimes asks the reader to read it again, to show them, yes, she meant to do that." (email from Lynne Savitt) Here's an example of the technique from *Blonde Blacklit By The Brooklyn Bridge*:

> "it wasn't me by the bridge but
> you smile teeth missing trouble
> breathing say again, "blonde
> i'll never forget," oh how i
> adored you broke my heart
> remembers who do you have
> me confused with my name"

and vivid description. She uses color and tone skillfully and naturally. Indeed, naturalism is central to her approach and also to her philosophy. She is a hedonist, and she isn't ashamed of it. Consequently, her poems are pleasurable to read and an escape from the mundane. She is daring in both word and deed, and this places her in that rarified category of openly-sexual women writers. It's a short, brave list: Sappho, Anaïs Nin, Erica Jong, Lynne Savitt. The new generation owes them a debt of gratitude.

This lengthy collection reads like a novel in poetry. Because the poems are autobiographical, and because they all deal with the struggle to love in one way or another, there is a consistent narrative in this collection that is rarely encountered in poetry. But, the writing isn't prosaic, because Lynne Savitt is a natural poet who writes for fundamentally therapeutic reasons. When I asked her if all her poems are true, her reply was that she thought that was how it was supposed to be. "Publishing is not important at all to me. The joy & fulfilment comes from the writing and the clarity, for me, is the reward." (email from Lynne Savitt)

She is not naive, however. She studied with Diane Wakoski. As a young poet she loved the poems of Anne Sexton, John Berryman and Pablo Neruda. Her biggest and earliest influence was Dorothy Parker.

Her functionalism does extend to her poems. Savitt isn't the poet for readers who are looking for a wide variety of innovative poetic techniques, but her limited repertoire of tricks is more than balanced by her psychological courage and her ability to magically convey her true conflicts into poetry. Her poems are very similar in tone and contain highly colorful imagery, but they are distinctive. One can immediately identify Lynne Savitt as their author after hearing a few bars, like the intro to a popular song that everyone recognizes. Savitt is capable of rocking out sensual imagery like few others. A few lines from her poem *The Deployment Of Love In Pineapple*

Twilight will illustrate:

> "camped at your tiny archway
> lit by yellow glowing candles
> sweet & sour as chinese pork
> i taste on your full wet mouth
> chopsticks red silk pajamas
> slim volumes of erotica save
> me intravenous they remove
> from my blue swollen
> hands in the midnight lime"

Savitt's whole approach to poetry is avant-garde in that she pushes the psychological boundaries in much the same way as Allen Ginsberg did in his time. Ginsberg insisted on candor in his poetry, and so does Savitt. Ginberg's work was an extension of the confessional poetry of Robert Lowell, combined with Blakeian mysticism and the long breaths of Whitman. Although firmly in the confessional camp, Savitt writes more in the 'personalist' mode of Frank O'Hara. Her poems, like O'Hara's, are 'in memory of my feelings.' The two poets are also similar in the integrative use of everyday imagery to color essentially autobiographical poems. O'Hara's work has a quality of having been written like a diary, as does Savitt's. They also share a painterly use of visual imagery and an entertaining personality that puts the poet at the center of the poem and makes them *fun* to read and easy to relate to.

In a sense, like O'Hara, she writes a kind of elaborate occasional poem. Thanksgivings, birthdays, New Year's Day, etc. all inspire poems, as do more personal occasions, like anniversaries of certain moments in a love affair, or milestones in her children's and grandchildren's lives. Many of the poems are also addressed directly to another person, usually a lover. Aging and the passage of time is one of the themes that these 'occasional poems' carry. In time we love and lose, but passion for life helps us time is one of the themes that these 'occasional poems' carry. In time we love and lose, but passion for life helps us survive. Again, these poems are functional, in more ways than one.

I asked her how she felt about several confessional poets. She liked Sexton as a young poet, but outgrew her. She never liked Plath. I feel the same way. Sexton struggled, while Plath seems always to give in to either anger or depression. Sexton was, like Savitt, more of a party girl. They share the same personal and poetic dilemma.

Savitt's work is erotic, which means *life-giving*. The great gift she has is that she can write for herself primarily while simultaneously expressing feelings that are universal, the longing for love and the human need to go a little crazy sometimes.

Darkened Rooms Of Summer - New And Selected Poems
by Jared Carter
(University of Nebraska Press, Lincoln, NE)

Jared Carter published his first poetry collection in his early forties. That book, *Work, for the Night is Coming* (Macmillan, 1981) won the prestigious Walt Whitman Award. The first poem in the book, from that collection, is *Geodes*. In its final couplet, Carter's lifelong theme is perfectly stated:

"I want to know only that things gather themselves
with great patience, that they do this forever."

Many ghosts and antiques occupy these poems. Jared Carter doesn't like to throw something valuable away. He presents us with a unique blend of lyric, narrative and philosophical values that evoke the past and its poetic forms. His poems are themselves instant antiques. To accomplish his restorative craft, the poet uses 'antiquated' methods, devices and structures. In one sense, the poems are pastiques, but Carter rescues them from being imitative by playing the ancient music as well or better than the poets who wrote it contemporaneously. Time itself becomes a secondary subject in nearly all the poems, as the poet works toward the timeless.

Many of Carter's finest poems seem inspired by overheard conversations, the kind you hear in small-town diners, bars, barbershops and feed stores. The poet listens to the stories of his neighbors and reports them. He lets the stories speak for themselves. They are the kind of stories that people remember and repeat, that imply a deeper meaning. Although he inspires easy comparison to Robert Frost, Edgar Lee Masters and Edwin Arlington

Robinson, Carter channels a stronger connection to Walt Whitman, whose democratic vision he shares. Like his influences, Carter is a true outsider, an outsider even to the other outsiders. His use of rhyme, formal structures like the villanelle and non-contemporary imagery makes him a true individualist. As noted previously, he doesn't like to throw away valuable antiques. He is a non-academic formalist and a revivalist, a rarity on the contemporary poetry scene.

I've always tried to be flexible, even neutral, in conflicts between the hip and the stiff. Reading and getting Carter's work requires such an open attitude. It may be helpful for the reader to regard it as a kind of folk poetry. Genuine eclecticism allows one to read beyond personal biases.

In his second collection, *After the Rain* (Cleveland State University Poetry Center, 1993), Carter hits his stride. He was in his fifties when it was published.

For me, the first truly moving poem in the book is *Foundling*. Here are the first and last stanzas of this five stanza poem:

Foundling

I would be safe there; she would look after me now.
When the car drove off, she showed me sweet
    alyssum
growing among the flagstones, and called it with
    names
learned form her own grandmother–madwort, heal-
    bite,
gold-dust, basket-of-gold. In the house, in the room
with the oak cupboard, I would have my own bed.
    Later,
when company came, and they thought I had fallen
    asleep,
I heard them speak of a love child in the

neighborhood,
whose parents had gone away. I wanted to
    mother.

* * *

Over the years I grew and prospered in that
    green place
always shining with light from the river, that
    world
that is gone now, under the waters, and can
    never return.
During the day I was joined with their stories;
    and once,
during feigned sleep, I heard those same voices
    whisper
the names of my real mother and father, who
    loved each other,
who left their mark on my own flesh, as one
    might draw
letters in the sandbank of a stream, or a fresh
    snowfall.
Over the years I remember the willows shading
    those walkways,
the gardens we tended, the flowers we gave to
    each other.

The above mentioned influences (Frost, Robinson, Masters) are more apparent in Carter's narrative poems than in his formal lyric works. The burden of rhyme may be the crucial dividing factor.

Barn Siding, also from *After the Rain*, is a major long poem and quintesssential Carter. There are one hundred and twenty-eight four-line stanzas. The narrator is a picker who accidentally pulls an old barn down on himself. He has time to think about his life while he lies trapped beneath the collapsed barn. He is finally saved, by an unexpected savior. Carter's ability to sustain the reader's interest over 512 lines is truly remarkable.

Each poem from *Les Barricades Mystérieuses* (Cleveland State University Poetry Center, 1999) is a villanelle. The villanelle is a very difficult form, because the repetition can be gratuitous, or sing-songy, thus off-putting to the reader. These are Carters least successful poems. None achieve the pure musicality infused with meaning of a great villanelle such as *Do Not Go Gentle Into That Good Night* by Dylan Thomas.   Readers who prefer high formalism may legitimately disagree with me. Sometimes I am uncomfortable with rigid form and have difficulty looking past it to its essence.

Cross This Bridge at a Walk (Wind Publications, 2006) goes back to Carter's long narrative mode. Another major long poem of over 400 lines, titled *Covered Bridge* follows the same pattern as the *Barn Siding* poem. Story-telling is Carter's great strength. *A Dance in the Street* (Wind Publications, 2012) continues in a similar folksy, narrative mode, playing to that strength.

The *New Poems* section of the book consists of formal, rhymed poems with single word titles like *Clouds, Moth, Graveyard* and *Perseus.* Carter uses Elizabethan phraseology and language that would fit comfortably in the King James Version. These poems are not Shakespeare, but they aim in that direction, a road less traveled in today's world.

The last lines from *Drawing the Antique* summarize the spirit of Carter's poetry:

> Yet we are shocked, we know them instantly–
> recognizable as victims everywhere, shapes
> destroyed and timeless,
>
> > still able to instruct."

An eclectic reader may find timeless value in *Darkened Rooms of Summer*. A poet should follow his heart before fashion, shouldn't he?

Thread Of The Real
by Joseph Hutchison
(Conundrum Press, Georgetown, Ontario)

At his best, Joseph Hutchison is capable of transcending ordinary perception to higher truths. He penetrates the surface of his subjects with a steady eye and a great ear. He is not afraid of the 'big subjects' of love, war and death. He takes a naturalistic approach, using clear, precise imagery and musical intonation to grapple with the ineffable.

Thread of the Real, published in 2012, contains two dozen or so excellent poems, along with other well-written poems that never fail to at least illuminate a truth. The minor poems can be either too prosaic or a bit trivial, but the major poems more than make up for this weakness with their absolutely gorgeous musicality and transcendental associative leaps. The first two sections of the book have several poems that illustrate these features. One of the best is *The Spring*, a poem that is both clear and deep.

The Spring

Your chest's like a grave
at a crossroads, and the dead
within it shiver: their spirits
rush . . . make your backbone
bend and dip like a hazel wand.

You touched your breast, told
the curious: "Here. Sink your well
here." The timid refused. But one
labored to split you open—worked
with teeth gritted against even
your own curses–and drew up,

in the end, buckets of shadow,
nothing but shadow . . .

Then others came, called
hopefully into your depths;
now only the echoes flow
inside you, moaning
in fear or delight–
who can say? But the ache
of that music makes you thirst,
bowing to the secret spring
you've never learned
to drink from.

Section III departs from the ecstatic and
transcendental approach of the first two sections to directly
address political and social problems. If simple clarity is
Hutchison's goal in his political poems, he has achieved it,
but the lack of metaphor, after its deft use in the previous
sections, is disappointing. The social poems are better than
the political poems, perhaps because they are more
personal. The best poem in this section is *Crossroads*, a
narrative about an encounter with 'a derelict' that goes
beyond simple narrative into interior monologue.

Section IV features two sequences of poems about
the poet's parents, who are both deceased. These are very
fine elegiac poems, from both aesthetic and emotional
perspectives. The sequence for his father, *The Mist of
Sustenance*, contains five short poems. The sequence for
his mother, *Comfort Food*, contains eight short poems.
Hutchison's strong feelings for his parents come through in
these touchingly evocative poems, while avoiding the overt
sentimentality that would have ruined them.

Section V contains several of the best poems in the
collection. The best poems in the book are *Wild Irises*,
dedicated to the poet's wife Melody, *Yoga* (also for Melody)
and *Unfinished Stories*, dedicated to his granddaughter.

These beautiful poems illustrate how Hutchison is at his very best in writing about people whom he truly loves.

The difference between the emotionally intense fifth section that contains strikingly evocative poems and the political and social poems of section three is revelatory, not only in regard to Hutchison's poetry, but also to the difference between personal and political poetry in general. Alan Tate, in a 1950 speech entitled *To Whom Is The Poet Responsible?*, had this to say:

> "I confess that the political responsibility of poets bores me; I am discussing it because it irritates me more than it bores me. It irritates me because the poet has a great responsibility of his own: it is the responsibility to be a poet, to write poems, and not to gad about using the rumor of his verse, as I am now doing, as the excuse to appear on platforms and to view with alarm."

Although I do not take as strict a view as Tate regarding political poetry, I do think that he identifies a dangerous vortex that poets can easily fall into when attempting to poeticize their politics. For the record, Hutchison's political views are 'correct' for the majority of liberal-leaning poets, myself included. I'm sure that Hutchison feels his politics strongly, but the intensity of his feelings for his wife and granddaughter far outweigh politics in their inspirational value to the poet and the reader, with the result that a poem such as *Wild Irises* arguably contains more real poetry than all the social and political poems of Section III.

Wild Irises

for Melody, again

Half asleep in the half-empty bed,
I touched your absence as I did
those ancient, troubled months
when I couldn't trust you'd ever
lie by me again–then lapsed

toward the dream that ached
like a hiding child's held breath.
Night. A lake. Restless winds.
The cloud-swaddled moon broke
through here and there, chalked

fragmentary ciphers on the ripples.
The scene like something turned up
in Tarot: a cloak-bowed wanderer,
his path pinched between dark water
and darker woods. Then a sudden

shift of cloud: brightness streams
from the moon's jade jar; the cloak
weighs my own shoulders down.
At my feet, wild irises–hundreds
swaying near and far in the radiance,

their petals thin as the veil
between this life and the next,
their scent your scent, their leaves
tracings of your body's curves. How
is it, I wonder, that I ever feel lost

when your beauty lies all around me?
And then I start off, down the path,
like a fresh line of verse–drawn
onward by onwardness, toward some
kind of waking, some end without end.

Writing a great love poem is extremely difficult. The essential element in such a poem is the depth of the love that inspired it, transfigured into imagery.

The final section, included for tongue-in-cheek comic relief after the love, death and war of the other sections, is in the same vein as the legendary book *The Tablets I-XV. Presented by the scholar-translator. Transmitted through Armand Schwerner.* Like Schwerner before him, Hutchison makes fun of obsessive-compulsive academia. He ends his collection with a statement: don't take things too seriously. Clear words from a passionate and talented poet.

Author Bio

Eric Greinke was born in 1948 in Grand Rapids, Michigan. He was educated at Grand Valley State University, with a B.A. in English and Psychology, and a M.S.W. in Clinical Social Work. He has produced numerous collections of poetry, a novel, a fishing book, two essay collections, a translation of Rimbaud and a collection of interviews. His work has been published widely in the U.S. and abroad in hundreds of literary magazines, such as the *California Quarterly, The Delaware Poetry Review, Gargoyle, Ginyu* (Japan), *The Green Door* (Belgium), *The Hurricane Review, The Journal* (UK), *Main Street Rag*, the *New York Quarterly*, the *Paterson Literary Review, The Pedestal Magazine, Poem, Prosopisia* (India), *The South Carolina Review* and *The University of Tampa Review.* He is one of twenty American poets included in *The Second Genesis - An Anthology of Contemporary World Poetry* (Anuraag Sharma, Ed.; Ajmer, India, 2014).

Website: www.ericgreinke.com.

Acknowledgments

Grateful acknowledgment is made to the publications that originally published these reviews:

Amaranthus, (Grand Valley State University, Allendale, MI): *The Yellow Room - Love Poems* by Donald Hall, (Harper & Row, New York, NY), Spring, 1972; **The Grand Rapids Press,** (Grand Rapids, MI): *Speech Acts & Happenings* by Robert Vas Dias, (Bobbs-Merrill Press, Indianapolis, IN), April, 1972; *A Caterpillar Anthology - A Selection Of Poetry And Prose From Caterpillar Magazine* edited by Clayton Eshleman, (Doubleday-Anchor Press, New York, NY), May,1972; *Shaking The Pumpkin - Traditional Poetry Of The Indian North Americas* edited by Jerome Rothenberg, (Doubleday-Anchor Press, New York, NY), June, 1972; *Smudging* by Diane Wakoski, (Black Sparrow Press, Los Angeles, CA), July, 1972; *Logan Stone* by D. M. Thomas, (Cape Golliard-Grossman Press, London, UK/New York, NY), July, 1972; *The Whispering Wind - Poetry By Young American Indians* edited by Terry Allen, (Doubleday-Anchor Press, New York, NY), August, 1972; *Mocking-Bird Wish Me Luck* by Charles Bukowski, (Black Sparrow Press, Los Angeles, CA), August, 1972; *Poems From Three Decades* by Richmond Lattimore, (Scribner Publishing, New York, NY), September, 1972; *Moving* by Tom Raworth, (Cape Golliard-Grossman Press, London, UK/New York, NY), October, 1972; *The Blue Cat* by F. D. Reeve, (Farrar, Straus & Giroux, New York, NY), October, 1972; *The Providings* by Carl Thayler, (Sumac Press, Fremont, MI), October, 1972; *The Revenant* by Dan Gerber, (Sumac Press, Fremont, MI), October, 1972; *Xeme* by Rebecca Newth, (Sumac Press, Fremont, MI), October, 1972; *Accidental Center* by Michael Heller, (Sumac Press, Fremont, MI), October, 1972; *Midwatch* by Keith Wilson, (Sumac Press, Fremont, MI), October, 1972; *A Day Book* by Robert Creeley, (Scribner Publishing, New York, NY), January, 1973; *My House* by Nikki Giovanni, (Harper-Perennial Press, New York, NY), January, 1973; *John's Heart* by Tom Clark, (Golliard-Grossman Press, London, UK/New York, NY), May, 1973; *New Work* by Joe Brainard, (Black Sparrow Press, Los Angeles, CA), December, 1973; **Home Planet News,** (High Falls, NY): *Light At The End - The Jesus Poems* by Lyn Lifshin, (Clevis Hook Press, Rochester, NY), 2009; *Something Is Burning In Brooklyn* by Linda Lerner, (Iniquity Press/Vendetta Books, Manasquan, NJ), 2009; *Nothing Divine Here* by Gloria Mindock, (Ušokuštampa, Cetinje and Montenegro & Springfield, VA), 2010; **The Pedestal Magazine,** (Charlotte, NC): *Hence This Cradle* by Hélène Sanguinetti, translated by Ann Cefola, (Otis Books/Seismicity Editions, Los Angeles, CA), June, 2007; *After Shakespeare - Selected Sonnets* by George Held, (Červená Barva Press, Somerville, MA), February, 2012; *Relics Of Lust: New & Selected Poems* by Lynne Savitt, (NYQ Books, New York, NY), September, 2014; *Darkened Rooms Of Summer* by Jared Carter, (University of Nebraska Press, Lincoln, NE), Spring, 2015; *Thread Of The Real* by Joseph Hutchison, (Conundrum Press, Georgetown, Ontario), Spring, 2015; **Presa**, (Rockford, MI): *The Winged Energy Of Delight* by Robert Bly, (Harper-Perennial Press, New York, NY), Fall, 2005; *They* by Spiel, (March Street Press, Greensboro, NC), Fall, 2007; *Inrue* by Guy Beining, (Phrygian Press, Bayside, NY), Spring, 2008; *Outside The End* by Guy Beining, (The Silver Wonder Press, Chicago, IL), Spring, 2008; *The Ristorante Godot* by Gerald Locklin, (Bottle of Smoke Press, Dover, DE), Spring, 2008; *Wedlock Sunday And Other Poems* by Gerald Locklin, (Liquid Paper Press, Austin, TX), Spring, 2008; *Think* by Mark Sonnenfeld, (Marymark Press, East Windsor, NJ), Spring, 2008; *London Nov 6 - Nov 11* by Mark Sonnenfeld, (Marymark Press, East Windsor, NJ), Spring, 2008; *Summer With All Its Clothes Off* by Art Beck, (Gravida, New York, NY), Spring, 2008; *Living Proof* by Mary Bonina, (Červená Barva Press, Somerville, MA), Spring, 2008; *Still Life* by Alan Catlin, (Black Buzzard Press, Austin, TX), Spring, 2008; *Among Us* by Harris Gardner, (Červená Barva Press, Somerville, MA), Spring, 2008; *Illegal Border Crosser* by Michael Graves, (Červená Barva Press, Somerville, MA), Spring, 2008;*Vanishing Points* by Gayle Elen Harvey, (The Sow's Ear Poetry Review, Milkwood, VA), Spring, 2008; *Blue Ribbons At The County Fair* by Ellaraine Lockie, (PWJ Publishing, Tehama, CA), Spring, 2008; *The Alchemy Of Words* by Edward Francisco, (Birch Brook Press, Delhi, NY), Fall, 2008; *The Republic Of Lies* by Ed Ochester, (Adastra Press, Easthampton, MA), Fall, 2008; *Ten Songs From Bulgaria* by Linda Nemec Foster, (Červená Barva Press, Somerville, MA), Fall, 2008; *A Very Funny Fellow* by Donald Lev, (NYQ Books, New York, NY), Spring, 2012; *The Devil's Sonata* by David Chorlton, (Future Cycle Press, Lexington, KY), Spring, 2013; *Drastic Dislocations - New And Selected Poems* by Barry Wallenstein, (NYQ Books, New York, NY), Spring, 2013.

Selected Presa Press Titles

John Amen
At The Threshold Of Alchemy
Guy Beining
Nozzle 1-36
Louis E. Bourgeois
Alice
Kirby Congdon
Selected Poems & Prose Poems
Athletes
Remarks And Reflections - Essays
Hugh Fox
Blood Cocoon - Selected Poems Of Connie Fox
Time & Other Poems
Eric Greinke
The Drunken Boat & Other Poems From The French Of
    Arthur Rimbaud
The Potential Of Poetry
Conversation Pieces - Selected Interviews
For The Living Dead - New & Selected Poems
Ruth Moon Kempher
Retrievals
Kerry Shawn Keys
The Burning Mirror
Book Of Beasts
Transporting, A Cloak Of Rhapsodies
Night Flight
Arthur Winfield Knight
High County
Champagne Dawns
Richard Kostelanetz
PO/EMS
More Fulcra Poems
Purling Sonnets
Linda Lerner
Living In Dangerous Times

Donald Lev
Only Wings - 20 Poems Of Devotion
Where I Sit
Lyn Lifshin
In Mirrors
Lost Horses
Glenna Luschei
Seedpods
Total Immersion
Witch Dance - New & Selected Poems
Sprouts
Leaving It All Behind
Gerald Locklin
From A Male Perspective
Deep Meanings - Selected Poems 2008-2013
Peter Ludwin
Rumors Of Fallible Gods
Gary Metras
The Moon In The Pool
Stanley Nelson
Pre-Socratic Points & Other New Poems
Limbos For Amplified Harpsichord
City Of The Sun
B. Z. Niditch
Captive Cities
Roseanne Ritzema
Inside The Outside - An Anthology Of Avant-Garde
American Poets
(includes: Kirby Congdon, Doug Holder, Hugh Fox, Eric Greinke, John Keene, Richard Kostelanetz, Lyn Lifshin, Richard Morris, Stanley Nelson, Lynne Savitt, Mark Sonnenfeld, Harry Smith, and A. D. Winans)
Lynne Savitt
The Deployment Of Love In Pineapple Twilight
Steven Sher
Grazing On Stars - Selected Poems
Harry Smith
Little Things
Up North (with Eric Greinke)
t. kilgore splake
Ghost Dancer's Dreams
Splake Fishing In America

Beyond The Ghosts
Winter River Flowing Selected Poems 1979-2014
Alison Stone
Dangerous Enough
Lloyd Van Brunt
Delirium - Selected Poems
Marine Robert Warden
Beyond The Straits
A. D. Winans
The Other Side Of Broadway - Selected Poems 1965-2006
Wind On His Wings
This Land Is Not My Land
Leslie H. Whitten Jr.
The Rebel - Poems By Charles Baudelaire

**For information about these and other titles,
please visit our website www.presapress.com.**

**Available through Baker & Taylor,
The Book House, Coutts Information Services,
Midwest Library Services, local bookstores
& directly from the publisher.**

**Exclusive European distribution through
Gazelle Book Service Ltd.
White Cross Mills, Hightown, Lancaster, LA1 4XS, UK
sales@gazellebooks.co.uk   www.gazellebooks.co.uk**

"Readers often mistakenly believe that to be 'good,' poetry must be written with exquisite, complex language, almost like the trills and other flourishes decorating Baroque music. However, as prize-winning poet, publisher, essayist, social worker and philosopher, Eric Greinke explains, in poetry, the enchanting, decorative quality of language represents ideas. This is Greinke at his best, advocating at the cutting edge of human growth in consciousness and doing it with poetry." - Ann Wehrman, *Poetry Now*

"For decades poet, small press innovator, and critic Eric Greinke has been working in poetry and with poetry, that is to say writing, publishing it, and probably most importantly, questioning the aesthetics that makes up the craft of verse, free or no." - Scott Whitaker, *The Broadkill Review*

"Greinke's clarity lets the reader in to what is being said, making it possible to apply, or at least, relate to these ruminations... "Open-mindedness of poets should at least be equivalent to that of musicians and painters. It is imperative for the growth of the poetic art that poets become more tolerant and eclectic readers, in deed."
- Irene Koronas, *Wilderness House Literary Review*